Lost in Goodland

Lost in Goodland:

A MEMOIR OF CHILDHOOD CHAOS

Jeremy Mills

Contents

Preface...5

Christmas 2001...9

The Good Years..15

Goodland..21

Divorce...29

The Fork in the Road..................................33

Isolation 39

Man of the House......................................43

Unraveling..47

The Return 55

Abandoned 59

The End of 240 Walnut 67

Escape to El Dorado 75

Jason & Kalyn 83

A Cold Night In Dodge City 87

Grandma & Nathan......................................97

Handy Towers 107

Escape To Rapid City 113

Do I Tear It All Down? 127

Basketball Date 133

Goodbye Goodland... 137

Seattle... 143

She's Gone 149

Afterimage 159

Making It Out... 167

Just Broken 175

In the End.. 183

To Mom

Preface

In June 1867, commanding from the newly established Fort Sedgwick in northeast Colorado, General William T. Sherman sent Lieutenant Lyman S. Kidder and his crew to deliver orders to Lieutenant Colonel George Custer.

While en route to Custer, Kidder's group got lost and were ambushed by Lakota and Cheyenne forces twenty miles northeast of Goodland. All twelve men were killed, then scalped. Their skulls were crushed, tendons cut, noses severed, and their bodies left pierced with arrows—a ritual to prevent their enemy from fighting from the afterlife.

To some, it was savagery; to others, it was a desperate act of survival in a world closing in on them.

Today, the site of the Kidder Massacre remains largely undeveloped, a stretch of plains and countryside much like it was in 1867.

Nearly twenty years later, in 1886, Sherman County was established. Goodland followed in 1887. Soon after, homesteaders began carving out their lives on the open plains, but the land wasn't easy to live on. Fires tore through the dry grass and floods rose quickly, swallowing everything in their path. The area seemed to offer nothing except sky and struggle.

In the early 20th century, Northwest Kansas saw a burst of expansion, fueled by wheat and hope. But that came at a cost. Overplowing tore up the deep-rooted native grasses that had once held the plains together, leaving the soil exposed and brittle. When the rain stopped and the winds returned, they didn't sweep across the land. They carried it away.

During the 1930s, the wind turned violent. Black clouds of dust swallowed the sky, reducing visibility to a few feet. Crops withered. Entire fields vanished. A decade of drought and erosion pushed families to their breaking point. Many left.

Those who stayed weren't necessarily tougher. Those who stayed weren't always stronger. They were just stuck. Too poor to leave and too proud to quit.

Fourteen miles south of modern-day Goodland, on the Dyatt family ranch, the land was mostly shortgrass prairie, a quiet patch traced by a winding branch of the Smoky Hill River. In the 1920s, the family built a dam, and turned a slow stretch of the river into a lake, and filled the land with boats, ball games, dances, and fireworks. That spot came to be known as Smoky Gardens.

On the Fourth of July, crowds swelled to the thousands. Families from all areas of Northwest Kansas and eastern Colorado loaded up clothes, tents, and fishing gear, setting out for a few days of camping under the prairie sky. They swam, they danced, and they made memories.

But year after year, the floods came.

The dam was washed out more than once. One storm after another tore through, flattening what they'd built, drowning what they'd planted. And still, they rebuilt. Again and again.

In 1936, a flood rolled in fast and violent, destroying bridges, roads, and farms. In its wake, it took the life of Mrs. Dyatt. The water rose so quickly that she was caught trying to escape. She died of shock, a devastating blow not only to the family, but to the Smoky as a whole.

The loss marked the beginning of a long decline. The dam failed, the lake drained out, and the Smoky slowly faded away. Though there were efforts in the '40s to revive it, red tape, more floods, and the hard math of rural survival kept it buried.

When my grandparents got there in the 1970s, it was hard to tell if there was any life left. But Grandpa Butts worked alongside others to restore and breathe life into the land once again. He planted oats on the silt fill for conservation, ensuring the soil remained stable. He used a tractor and chain to transplant young cottonwood trees from nearby, planting them along the south side of the Smoky with the hope of providing shade for someone in the future who needed a quiet place to sit and rest.

It is within this landscape that my own story unfolds. Where the past echoes. Sometimes heavy, sometimes faint, but it lingers all the same. Begging me to understand, to release, and to move forward.

My family carried this heaviness quietly, passing down the wounds they hid through generations.

Trauma is not merely a memory. It's a weight we live with. It settles deep in our bones, lingers in our blood, and weaves itself into our DNA. The land remembers too. The earth holds the weight of what has come before.

This isn't a heaviness I can carry anymore. But I can't leave it behind either. So, I am releasing it in an attempt to lift the burden from my chest and heal my heart.

The last thing I want is to put my mother down or expose our family's struggles, but I've spent twenty years protecting others. These memories have haunted and weighed me down, occupying my mind and holding me back. If you've ever carried the weight of memories that refuse to stay silent, you'll understand why I had to write this. It took years of therapy, journaling, and meditation to get to this point, but it wasn't enough.

I know some of you reading have been through worse. Maybe you're still in it. Maybe you've never had the chance to say it out loud. If there's any point to this, it's to show that the past does not have to define you. Speaking your truth, even when it hurts, is a way forward. Maybe even a way out.

CHAPTER ONE

Christmas 2001

I didn't have the words for it. My brain had not developed enough to understand, but I could feel *something*. Pressure building, a thunderstorm gathering in the distance. Cold and electric. The kind which turns day to night.

My reaction as an eight-year-old was to be upset with my brother's defiance. It scared me to see him so pissed off with Mom, and it deeply troubled me to see her upset. More than anything, I needed him to be wrong. But deep in my heart, I knew he wasn't.

I'd check the time, sure it had been hours, only to find a handful of minutes had passed. The knot in my gut tightened with every passing moment. Dad was coming home soon, and when he did, the truth would come to light. I wasn't scared of my dad. I was scared of the clarity he would bring and what it would mean for our family.

Recently, strange people had started coming to our house to spend time with Mom while Dad was out of town for work, replacing the extended family members that we would normally see.

I was uneasy and confused about why she was hanging around them, but naivete and a deep well of empathy for her colored my outlook. Keeping peace in the family and seeing her happy was all I cared about, especially because of how devastating the alternative was. But I couldn't deny these new people were unsettling.

Their faces were marked by a life lived fast and hard, appearing decades older than they really were. Deep wrinkles were etched across their faces. A restless, almost desperate urgency flickered in their eyes. They would show up buzzed and leave wasted, if they left at all.

When they were there, before we were sequestered in our room, some would talk to my brothers and me. Some tried to trick us into thinking we knew them, or that we were safe around them. Others didn't bother. They looked right through us.

Often, these strangers would get too close, some with a harsh chemical odor on their breath, and speak in slurred, confusing fragments that we couldn't make sense of. Sometimes it carried an ominous undertone; other times it was rude and nonsensical.

I didn't know it, but I'd spend a decade trying to untangle what these kinds of people would do to me.

Mom would transform into a different person when she was around them. She was no longer the sweet, uncomplicated beacon of love that us boys were used to. A reckless intensity would start to take over, her voice rising in both volume and certainty. Her boastful laughter lacked warmth, because deep down, all of this was fueled by a broken heart.

Her father died of skin cancer a few years earlier, likely from too much time spent farming under the Kansas sun. As time passed, nights where I would find her alone, crying on the side of her bed became a regular occurrence. The raw emotion in her sobs was heart-wrenching, not only in the moment, but to this day, twenty years later, as it involuntarily replays in my mind.

"I just miss him," she would mutter between sobs, if she could get anything out at all.

It was easy for a young boy to understand. The anger from my oldest brother was more complex. Johnathan was fourteen years old and much more aware of the situation than I was. Our other brother, Josh, was thirteen and stuck somewhere in the middle.

Johnathan couldn't contain his feelings about what she was doing and challenged her. Despite Mom's vehement denials, he knew something was terribly wrong. With a ruthlessness we hadn't seen before, she psychologically manipulated him into questioning his own reality. Demanding there was nothing wrong with what she was doing, Mom was quick to cast him as an angry teenager, framing it in a way that cast doubt on the allegations that trickled out to our extended family. That gaslighting made him doubt his own intuition, second-guessing as if it could all be in his head—a scar damned to linger.

Mom tried to save face within her immediate and extended family, keeping the lie of normalcy going on as long as possible, either blind or uncaring to the mental and emotional damage it was causing to her children.

But a storm was coming. And none of us were ready. The veil of denial was about to be ripped away. With Dad's return, the truth would come out. Mom would be facing someone older, and far less susceptible to her manipulations.

During the last few months, I'd been tormented by a recurring dream. I was sitting on a silent, condemned Earth. No birds. No breeze. Nothing but stillness so absolute that it pressed against my eardrums.

Then I would see it. Off in the distance. An enormous asteroid hurtling directly towards me.

Worst of all, I knew I was the cause of it.

I don't know how I knew. But there was no doubt.

I'd be picking flowers in an eerily peaceful field, the knowledge of imminent destruction then completely paralyzing me. The serene beauty only amplified the horror of what was to come. The horror wasn't in chaos. It was in the quiet.

And then I'd be awake. Drenched in sweat. Struggling to shake off the terror that wrapped itself around me.

When Dad finally came home, we heard his rental car ease into the driveway and saw the glow of the headlights spill across the living room walls.

My heart dropped.

Johnathan, Josh, and I sat together in the living room, frozen in place on the same blue couch where we'd made so many memories. Where we used to sit as a family watching *The Simpsons* and *King of the Hill*, or where Mom and Dad would take over our PlayStation to play *Madden*. It was always Broncos vs. Packers.

"Bubba Franks!" Dad would proudly say after a big play to his tight end.

It was the same couch we sat on the day we first got that PlayStation and spent hours playing *Tony Hawk's Pro Skater*. The same couch I ran to after cheap-shotting Josh during one of our backyard wrestling matches, before he found me and broke my forearm with a flying knee.

It happened fast—Dad was home, and from down the hall our parents' voices tore through the walls.

They were arguing at a level we hadn't heard before. It wasn't the sound of a fight. It was the ground shifting under us.

The air hung heavy, thick with tension, and poisoned with hate. Twinkling Christmas lights mocked us. The neatly wrapped presents underneath the tree were cruel reminders of a happiness that was just out of reach.

We didn't look at each other. We didn't speak. We just sat there, three brothers in the glow of the tree, trying not to breathe too loud while our world fell apart one room away.

Mom came out of the room seething with rage and her eyes swollen from crying. An undeniable look of brokenness and fury enveloped her face. As angry as she looked, there was a child buried in her eyes, crying out for help.

I don't know if she grabbed me or I followed, but we got in the Suburban and for the first time, sought refuge at Grandma's. To me, it was a temporary escape—what else could it be? I didn't realize we were already choosing sides.

Before I knew it, I was on Grandma's couch, replaying the fresh memories of what just happened.

Dad was never violent with me. I can't even remember him raising his voice at us. But after the intensity of that night, clinging to my childhood brain, in the quiet of Grandma's house, I worried he was going to smash the Christmas present I'd been lusting after for so many months.

Over the last year or so, all me and my brothers did was skate. We spent the majority of our free time riding the streets of Goodland in search of new makeshift ramps, often the sides of a curb, or trying to land the three-stair jump at the junior high school. The Christmas present I'd been craving was the signature cobalt blue deck of my favorite skateboarder, Bob Burnquist.

The rest of the night was a blur. I mostly remember muffled crying, a low hum from the heater, and the feeling that we weren't supposed to be there. Not only because our family had fractured, but because Mom hated having to seek shelter there; the shame was clear in her eyes.

My body was braced for the truth, chest tight, breath held. But my mind wasn't ready.

The enormity of it all was too much for me to understand as an eight-year-old, but the crushing dread that washed over me was undeniable.

That night marked the quiet funeral of our little family.

It was the last time we'd all exist under the same roof. Nothing would be the same again.

Not the house.

Not the family.

Not me.

Not ever again.

CHAPTER TWO

The Good Years

In the years prior to this, my brothers and I spent the mornings before school with the scent of frozen waffles in the toaster, then meticulously cut into squares before they came to us, and the sound of morning cartoons on the TV.

Our stay-at-home mom was fiercely dedicated to raising us three boys. Her love was limitless and confidence-inspiring. Her embrace was the first place that I ever belonged. It was tight but never smothering. The kind of shelter that made the rest of the world disappear.

Aside from the morning waffles, she normally prepared healthy meals, not allowing us to leave the table until all the vegetables were finished. She taught us the importance of manners and treating people the right way. She read to us every night before tucking us in and telling us, "sweet dreams." In those days, I couldn't imagine going to sleep without hearing her say those words.

We lived in a nice home at 240 Walnut. Complete with a front yard, accented by two beautiful flower beds and a young tree we had planted as a family when we first moved in. In the backyard, we had a basketball goal and a sizable garden that Mom and Dad lived for.

We grew up with pets. We had Chip, our golden retriever-chow mix, and a kitten for every one of us boys, each one named and claimed as our own. I named mine "JC"–Jeremy's Cat.

Travel was a big part of Dad's work in telecommunications, so he was away a lot. Every two weeks, he returned home, sometimes for a weekend, now and then for a whole week, before returning to the road.

While he was home, his priority was hanging out with us. The entire family would go across the street to the park and play football and basketball. After, Dad would go inside and start cooking his signature stew, recruiting one of us to sort beans, picking out any stones or broken pieces. We'd take short trips in the summer to the Bonny Lake in Colorado. He would play music for us in the car, like Rush, repeating certain lyrics to emphasize their wisdom. I would demand to hear my anthem, "Jeremy" by Pearl Jam.

Nearly twenty years earlier, my parents first met at a bar along Highway 24 in Goodland. Dad was seismographing for an oil exploration crew. After becoming tired of wading through Louisiana's swamps, he decided to join a crew traveling through the Midwest instead.

Originally from Cordova, Alabama, a small town of about 2,000 people, Dad used music as a means of self-discovery from a young age, finding his way into the counterculture of the original hippie movement as a young adult in the early seventies.

He hitchhiked through the South with just his thumb and a bag. Among other places, he spent a transformative few days at The Farm, an intentional community near Summertown, Tennessee, where those invited to join the community faced a stark choice: stay for three days or commit for life. He was tempted, but he chose the former. Still, the influences stayed with him. Zen Buddhism left the deepest mark.

Dad found his way out of Cordova in his early twenties, working for the seismograph crew.

Mom was a Goodland native and the one sister among her four brothers. From oldest to youngest, it was Mike, Rod, Patty, Tony, and Troy.

Her dad, Neil, and his family were farmhands and lived a simple life, canning a lot of their own food and making some of their own clothes by hand.

Fourteen miles south of Goodland lies Smoky Gardens, a recreational area where my grandparents served as caretakers and my mom and her brothers grew up. In the early 1900s, before the Butts family became caretakers, The Smoky had already lived and died more times than anyone could keep track of. Built, abandoned, fought for, and rebuilt, only to be lost again.

For my mom and her brothers, it was home. The family house stood nearby, alongside a small farm, the fishing pond, campsites, picnic tables, barbecues, and playground. It was their whole world.

Mom often talked about a childhood shaped by farm work, waking up early to tend to animals, though shamefully I can't remember which ones. She talked about how her brothers bullied her. She saw them bully each other too, each with their own style of preferred torment.

As she got older, she said boys in town were afraid to talk to her because of the Butts boys' reputation for fighting. What was a joke at first genuinely seemed to have bothered her. I grew up on stories about their brawls. Troy, spin-kicking someone across a pool hall. Or Rod, ripping a guy's ponytail clean off. Or later, Mike, an imposing 6'4" and 250 pounds, stepping in when my dad was about to get jumped in a bar bathroom, lifting two men by their shirt collars and carrying them out. On the other side of that, Mom had been married once before, but with the help of her brothers, she escaped the physically abusive relationship.

Eventually, the kids grew up, my grandparents retired and moved to town, and The Smoky started to fade out again. By the time I was a teenager, it was completely dry.

After meeting my mom, Dad stayed in Goodland and started attending school at the Vo-Tech and a year later, Mom would be pregnant with my oldest brother Johnathan. After he was born in 1986, Dad's work took the little family to Texas, where Josh was born a year later, and then to Colorado, where I was born in 1993.

Dad wore his hair long, almost to the middle of his back. It wasn't curly but wavy, dark brown, and usually tied back in a well-kept ponytail. His tanned skin, which didn't seem to fade, perfectly matched his deep brown eyes. His aura was perfectly steady, calm energy, never rattled or overly excited. He was tall and skinny, yet strong from work, and his giant hands seemed big enough to curl up and go to sleep in.

I don't believe I ever saw him in a t-shirt. It was usually a short-sleeved collared shirt and blue jeans, which he'd buy thick and warm in the winter, then cut into weathered shorts by summer.

Mom was thin, with high cheekbones and straight, light brown hair. I definitely saw her wear t-shirts. Her style was effortlessly cool, a perfect reflection of '90s fashion. Her signature look included a blue denim fanny pack, a simple graphic tee, usually from a national park we'd visited, simple brown sunglasses, and a scrunchie.

She was as strong and stubborn as a cottonwood tree battered by the relentless Northwest Kansas wind, yet still standing. Her eyes were blue with a softness that could turn sharp in an instant. She had a natural beauty, casual and unassuming. More than that, she was authentic and sweet. Someone you couldn't help but want to protect and who was easy to love.

Within the year, we left Colorado and moved to the setting for the majority of our story. Tucked right into the northwest corner of the state, roughly nineteen miles east of the Colorado border and thirty-two miles south of Nebraska's border, is a town named Goodland, Kansas. I'll come back to that.

Looking back, the mid '90s were idyllic and the last stretch of calm before everything cracked. My Grandpa spent most of my earliest years with me, showering me with pure love. I spent so much time on his lap sleeping or hanging out in his shop while he worked, just being his little buddy. I was genuinely interested in what he was doing, and he lit up getting to show me. He bought me my first wrestling toys, companions that would keep me company through the hardest times. It was a two-pack: Kane and The Undertaker. I walked through the back door and spotted the package sitting between his and Grandma's chairs. He knew I saw it. I tried to play it cool. So did he. Then he casually handed it over and said he got it for his "Little Man."

When Grandpa was 18, he was hit by a car while riding a motorcycle, causing severe damage to his left arm that later required amputation. The missing arm didn't hinder him. Some of my earliest memories are watching him tie his boots one-handed, and hanging out in his garage watching him work as a mechanic.

Stories floated around about how strong his remaining arm was, how no one in the tri-state area could beat him at arm wrestling. While sitting idle, he often stretched rubber bands with his hand. Whether it was for exercise or to distract himself from the phantom pains of his missing arm was never clear.

Most notably were his overalls. Every day. My favorite was his blue-and-white pinstripe Key brand, though to me, they weren't overalls. They were "Grandpa Pants."

He died in September 1999 at 67 years old of skin cancer. Not only was he my number one, he was the anchor of the Butts family, and kept us connected. We didn't talk about it much, but you could see it, how his absence shaped us, decade after decade.

Lucky for me, there was already a strong bond between the Mills brothers. Josh and Johnathan were closer in age and definitely had the strongest connection. They were rarely referred to by their names, most often as "The Boys".

Johnathan's dark brown hair framed a kind, innocent face, with blue eyes that gave him an air of warmth and thoughtfulness. He was known as the smart one, often quizzing our older cousins on dinosaur names and even created and taught a class for me before I started kindergarten. Quiet by nature, it often seemed his mind was constantly working, carefully mulling over the situation. His silence wasn't from a lack of opinion, but from a tendency to speak only when he truly cared, for example during the 2000 election, when George Bush's victory became clear, and he stormed out of the room, shouting, "God damnit!"

Josh's hair was dark too, but softly curled, and a bit wild. His eyes were a deep brown, like our dad's. Whatever it is that makes us who we are as Mills, Josh got the most of it and in its purest form. He is unique among the unique. Truly his own person, in ways that are both obvious on the surface and deep and unexpected, offering insights into life and the world that you won't find anywhere else. He also has a streak of defiance and rebellion that comes with his independence; he'd rather carve his own path and face the struggles that come with it than follow someone else's.

As brothers, we'd immerse ourselves into our own world, like the elaborate play-wrestling league, complete with characters and storylines dreamt up mostly by Johnathan and Josh. Entrance music elevated the atmosphere, and custom-made trading cards and special attire added a touch of professional flair and world building. We would execute their moves in dramatic performances that ended in very real injuries from time to time.

I was the youngest and the smallest, but that didn't mean I was defenseless. I had my ways of evening the odds. My weakness in a fight became my strength in front of Mom. Especially at first, I got sympathy, so I would run to home base. When that wasn't an option, with all my might and muster, I'd unleash an incredible, high-pitched, high-powered shriek that stopped them in their tracks and got the attention of nearly everyone on the block.

My brothers were *the* main characters in my life, even then, while I was very young, I had a life going already.

CHAPTER THREE:

Goodland

Before we get too far into the story, it might help to take a step back and see where all of this took place.

Goodland, Kansas, is a small town surrounded by wheat fields and open plains stretching for miles. Rows of giant grain elevators and a few water towers overlook the town, nearly the only things breaking up the vast, open sky. As Truman Capote said, "It's a lonesome area that other Kansans call 'out there.'"

Goodland feels different from the rest of Kansas. Nothing like the populated eastern side. Technically, we're the highest county seat in the state—elevation-wise, anyway. That extra height brings stronger winds, heavier snow, and maybe a bit of a complex. The small things set us apart. While the rest of Kansas runs on Central Time, we're on Mountain Time.

Sherman County was established around 1886, and Goodland followed a year later in 1887, thanks to the railroads cutting through town and the homesteaders who settled the land.

One of the first families to arrive in March 1887 were my ancestors, Thomas and Margaret Butt (later Butts), who homesteaded on the SE 1/4 of Section 35, Township 9, Range 39 in Goodland.

Many of the early homes in Goodland were built by Thomas, one of the first carpenters in the area. Before that, he fought for the Union in the Civil War. He served as a bugler and took part in several key battles, including the capture of Island No. 10, a major strategic point for the Confederates.

He was part of a fleet of small boats that carried out a daring attack during the campaign. Wounded but alive, Thomas was discharged on July 7th, 1865. When he died in 1907, the Goodland Republic wrote, "An old landmark has fallen."

Back in 1886, there were four different communities in a dispute over who would be named the county seat of Sherman County:

Itasca, Voltaire, Sherman Center, and Eustis.

Then the idea is pitched for starting a brand-new town to settle the dispute.

That town would be called Goodland.

When it came time to vote, Goodland took it by a landslide. Eustis didn't take the loss well. They said the vote was unfair, tried to stir things up, but the state basically shrugged. The Kansas Supreme Court looked into it too, but didn't overturn anything. The votes were in. Goodland had won.

But Eustis wouldn't release the county records. That lasted until January 13th, 1888, when a few residents from Goodland had enough. They rolled into Eustis, armed and ready, raided the courthouse, and brought the books and records back with them. From that moment on, Goodland became the county seat.

Bruce Bair, in his memoir *Good Land: My Life as a Farm Boy*, describes the topography of Sherman County as lying atop an ancient alluvial fan. Layers of sediment washed down from the Rocky Mountains over millions of years, spreading out in a fan-like pattern, creating a foundation of gravel and sand.

After an unusually wet period in the area led white settlers to believe the area's climate was now different and that "the rain follows the plow."

During this era, Goodland saw its share of chaos and progress. Both prairie and building fires were common, along with brutal blizzards, railroad accidents, labor strikes, and the occasional train or bank robbery. Disease outbreaks among horses and cattle made ranching more difficult, and nearly twenty local deaths were recorded during the 1918 Spanish flu.

Still, the settlers kept building—from barns and wells to churches, schools, and a jail.

Overplowing during the Wheat Boom displaced the deep-rooted native grasses that had previously trapped soil and moisture during drought and high winds. Without enough rain to hold the loess in place, the same winds that once shaped the land stripped it bare, turning rich ground into dust.

During the drought of the 1930s, that now-unanchored dust rose into giant clouds during dust storms, sometimes cutting visibility down to three feet. Some of those clouds were so massive they reached the East Coast. Long stretches of dry weather caused crops to fail, leaving the plowed fields vulnerable to wind erosion. Entire fields were blown away. A decade of this ravaged the area and tested the resolve of the farmers who stayed.

The wind in Northwest Kansas doesn't stop. It pushes and pulls, wild and relentless, tearing through everything. My dad, most eloquently, summed up the area as "windy-ass, miserable Kansas." Occasionally, the wind turns feral, spawning a tornado that tears the plains apart.

After the Dust Bowl, the area survived and adapted the best it could. The underground water of the Ogallala Aquifer allowed farmers to survive and the Rock Island Railroad kept them connected with the rest of the country. It brought goods, news, people, and opportunity. At its peak, the railroad ran passenger services such as the *Rock Island Rocket*, linking Goodland to Kansas City and Denver in just a few hours. Even Presidents William H. Taft and Dwight D. Eisenhower passed through town on its rails.

In the 1940s, the one-room schools that had once been the norm across the area started to close. Farms got bigger. Machines did heavy lifting. And families, one by one, were moving to cities in search of work and opportunity.

After a sugar beet factory opened in the 1970s, Mexican immigrants planted their roots in town and made up almost the entire labor force within the industry, working hard to contribute to their new community.

In 1975, in a major blow to the area, the Rock Island Railroad declared bankruptcy. By 1980, the last train had run, and Goodland's once-busy depot went quiet.

The Kyle Railroad came in and took over, but unlike the grand passenger lines of the past, Kyle was strictly freight. Regional, agricultural, and bare-bones. No more travelers. No more Rocket. But it kept the grain moving and that was enough to survive.

The ups and downs continued for the area, with an especially low period during the droughts and the farming crisis of the 1980s. When their investments went belly up after demand slowed, many family farms did not survive, devastating not only those families, but the communities that were built around them. Some left and found better lives. Some stayed and tried to help develop better lives.

The 1990s brought challenges to the area. Small towns kept shrinking as residents left in search of better opportunities. Between 2000 and 2010, Goodland's population dropped by 8.64%, part of a larger trend of rural depopulation across the country.

Today, with a population of around 4,500, Goodland is mostly white, with a significant Hispanic community. According to the 2020 census, nearly a quarter of Goodland's population is under 18, and a sizable portion is over 65, which leaves fewer people in the middle to carry the load. Cattle farming, pinto beans, soybeans, corn, milo, and wheat are the backbone of the area. As one local leader told me, "If agriculture does well, the community is successful."

When I picture the classic Goodlandite, I imagine someone who takes pride in the simplicity of life, their family, and the traditions passed down through a few generations. While their small Kansas town may not offer much, they make the most of what they have and often feel no need to leave.

High school athletics, the Goodland Cowboys and Cowgirls, are a cornerstone of the community. At the top of the list are football and wrestling. The spirit of high school sports and the energy on a Friday night game day are as heartfelt and genuine as it gets. The smell of burgers on the grill, the marching band warming up, the crisp fall air, kids with black and gold face paint, parents and grandparents cheering in the stands, and the sound of crunching pads. Together, they create a sensory experience that has lingered in my memory for decades.

For wrestling, the Holiday Classic Tournament reigns supreme as a marquee event of the area at The Max Jones Fieldhouse, a beloved Goodland venue. The only thing that boosted your reputation more than excelling at football was having a reputation as a 'damn good wrestler.' That wasn't a high school thing—it started long before with *Kansas Kids* wrestling.

Growing up, The Max had a special energy for events, with the community coming out in full support. To us, it might as well have been Madison Square Garden.

The building is filled with history, honoring past athletes, including Brook Berringer, the star quarterback from Goodland who played collegiately at Nebraska, who lost his life in a plane crash two days before the 1996 NFL Draft. Along with a service at Nebraska's Memorial Stadium, Berringer's funeral was held at The Max Jones Fieldhouse.

The Max is a hotspot in town, a place you wanted to be growing up, as was Main Street.

The brick road on Main Street is famous in Goodland, not only for the activity it hosts but for its history. "Indian Jim," Jim Brown, is credited with laying the bricks in 1921, his skills still a legend passed down through the ages. According to the *Johnson County Democrat*, Indian Jim won a bricklaying competition by paving more than 416 feet of road with 46,664 eight-pound bricks in under eight hours, 1,755 more bricks than his opponent.

Those bricks later became part of the backbone for classic businesses like the Sherman Theatre, China Gardens, Crazy R's, Cowboy Loop, Garrett's Liquor Store (and Garrett's Laundromat), BankWest, the VFW, and the Goodland Activities Center, which was our version of the YMCA.

Perhaps the most quintessential activity a young person in Goodland would do was 'dragging Main.' High schoolers would flood Main Street in their pickups, cruising up and down, waving at friends or flipping off enemies, before gathering at the parking lot of the Cowboy Loop gas station, often another hub of activity.

On the surface, Goodland is a nice, clean place to raise a family. The kind of town where you can leave your keys in the car and your front door unlocked at night.

But there is another side. A side where those who don't fit the mold of the classic Goodlandite are ostracized, or judged as less worthy than someone with a well-established last name. A side where people desperately *do* want to leave, but are trapped, with no tangible way to escape. Where some people do want help, but there are minimal local resources for mental health and addiction.

I was never quite like most of the other kids in Goodland. Take, for example, the county fair when I was in middle school. There were carnival rides, game booths, food, and kids showing off their 4-H animals. Nearby at the racetrack, there were bull rides, stock car races, tractor pulls—and the one I'm leading up to: goat tying.

I sat alone in the stands, watching as children, urged on by their parents, would tackle a goat who was tied to a stake in the ground. Then they wrenched its neck and tried to tie its legs while the goat let out a blood-curdling cry. Those cries sounded eerily human. The poor thing thrashed wildly in a desperate attempt to escape.

I looked around, wondering if anyone else shared my reaction, but no one blinked an eye. So I spoke up, "Doesn't anyone else think this is wrong?"

Instead of any semblance of understanding or empathy, they yelled homophobic slurs, laced with the same vitriol they reserved for anyone that was different than them. Not an ounce of self-reflection, not a hint of doubt that they could be wrong.

Another reason stems from practice at *Kansas Kids Wrestling*. I don't remember exactly how young I was, but I know my brothers were living with me, so probably six or seven at most.

We'd gather in the evening at the Junior High gymnasium, the mats already laid out as parents and kids warmed up, moving with the ease of people who'd done this before. People who belonged. I was paired with another kid my size, and we started practicing drills. Several coaches roamed around, offering tips. The one nearest to us wore a baseball cap, with a white mustache, and glasses. From how I saw it, he was someone who fit in, not only in the gym, but in Goodland.

One of the other coaches came to me and my opponent, offering some tips, and abruptly grabbed my genitals, saying, "This! This is how you do it."

I wasn't old enough to fully understand how wrong it was, but I knew it made me incredibly uncomfortable and embarrassed. I already felt like I didn't belong. That sealed it.

In Goodland, from my experience, standing out often meant getting othered. From as early as I can remember, it was obvious to me that my family was different on a core level, both in who we were and how we were perceived. We didn't go to church, didn't farm, didn't hunt, didn't drive a pickup, didn't listen to country music, didn't wear baseball caps. Dad loved reading about Native American history and would take us to powwows in Denver, while most of our peers were busy with 4-H. More than that, we really just kept to ourselves.

In middle school, I wore black nail polish, which knocked me down a level socially. In junior high, I wore women's jeans and t-shirts, which were hand-me-downs from my brothers in the city, because they fit my slender frame better than the baggy clothes passed down from other relatives. That, too, knocked me down a peg. When I mentioned my interest in Buddhism, another student gave me a puzzled look, insisting it wasn't a *real religion*.

As a kid, those differences were stark, and I was firmly rooted in who I was. By high school, sports had helped bridge some of those gaps. Football brought a lot of us closer together.

During the lead-up to the 2008 presidential election, when I voiced my support for Barack Obama, the backlash reminded me how different we really were. I heard all of the conspiracies: he wasn't born in America, he was a Muslim, the Antichrist, and that white people would become slaves under his presidency.

In high school, around 2010, I gave a presentation in World History class on why gay marriage should be legal. Two separate classmates gave presentations and argued the opposite, and our teacher sided with them, citing reasons like, "If we let them get married, what's next? Dogs and cats?"

What it all adds up to is this: I felt like I didn't belong in Goodland.

The popular kids in school were from well-off farming families, deeply rooted in the community. I'm not sure if they were accepted for who they were or for what they represented. Previous generations of the Butts were farmers, but my last name isn't Butts. And as a skinny weird kid, I was pretty worthless on a farm.

In small communities like Goodland, following tradition means survival, and breaking the mold makes you a target. I didn't know it at the time, but my experience was not unique.

CHAPTER FOUR

Divorce

Despite my worries that night, I got my blue Bob Burnquist skateboard, unbroken.

I don't know when, or under what circumstances, but Mom and I returned to 240 Walnut and Dad went back on the road. Johnathan remained upset. Josh was upset too, but also confused, leaving him trapped in limbo. All I wanted was for life to be normal again. I clung to the illusion of stability, blinding myself to the growing cracks in the foundation.

One seemingly ordinary afternoon, Mom proposed that her and I go visit a house with a hot tub. I quickly agreed. When we arrived, there waiting to greet us was a person I hadn't met before.

He wore a baseball cap, his straight long brown hair poking through the back, semi-rimless baseball-style sunglasses, the kind you'd see on a baseball coach or hanging on a gas station rack, and a rough cut-off t-shirt.

His face was narrow and weathered, with deep lines around his mouth and forehead, the kind that settle in from years of scowling at the sun. His mustache sat thin and uneven, not quite covering the space above his mouth. When he took off his sunglasses, his eyes were brown but washed-out, sitting deep under a heavy brow, holding a constant intensity, a low voltage running behind them.

When he took his shirt off to get into the hot tub, I noticed a large scar going all the way down the middle of his torso. He later told me, in so many words, that two men broke into his house while he was living in Texas, and he was stabbed more than twenty-five times. It was the first I'd ever heard someone say the N-word.

The person I met that day became a regular presence. I later learned his name was Paul.

The parties at 240 Walnut intensified as the house became a revolving door for the riffraff of Goodland.

All of us brothers were banished to our rooms, now outcasts in our own home, while Mom and the strangers blasted music, yelled, and drank beer deep into the night. That's what we believed, anyway.

In the wee hours of the morning, fueled by frustration and confusion, we'd each take turns venturing out, pleading for quiet, but would be chastised and sent back to our rooms.

Lying in bed listening to a drunken party bleeding from the living room was annoying enough, but inevitably that would end, and Mom and Paul would be the only two left. Their yelling would become aggressive and confrontational. Whatever the worst possible thing they could say to each other would come out. Violent threats only became more extreme. The fury vibrated throughout the house, threatening to ignite with every jab.

With my mind racing and the constant noise pounding in my ears, sleep was impossible. My instincts urged me to help my mom, but her anger wasn't only for Paul. It was for anyone in sight. All we could do was endure, letting the weight of it all sink into our bones.

A few days would have been enough, but days turned to weeks, and things were only getting worse. Mom was defiant, not willing to entertain our questioning about what was going on.

Then, one afternoon, Mom gathered us three boys in the living room and motioned for us to sit on the couch. There was no television playing in the background, no music to mask the silence, it was as if the entire world were holding its breath.

I sat there, nerves tangled with a fragile hope: maybe she would finally apologize, tell us she was feeling like herself again, and that Dad would soon return to our old life.

My hands clenched the fabric of the seat as I braced for what was to come.

In that moment, my mind drifted to a cold morning in late September 1999. I was walking into this same living room, half-awake and rubbing my eyes to find Mom perched on this same couch.

"Is there no school today?" I asked.

With every ounce of strength she had, she muttered that "Grandpa passed away."

I'd never heard that term before, but the heaviness in her voice made its meaning undeniable. The room was transformed. Not in some dramatic way, but in the simple details: the carpet had a dry, scratchy feel, soft in the middle but with stiff edges that pressed into my feet. The low buzz of the fridge stood out—one of those things you only notice when the hum of everyday life suddenly stops.

This was the same living room where, on Christmas morning, barefoot and in our pajamas, we tore into our presents. One year, the gift was a keyboard; Josh jumped right in, as if he'd been playing for years. Another year, all three of us had to work together to open the new basketball hoop for the backyard.

Back on the couch, Mom began to speak and the hope I'd been holding onto slipped away. Her voice, worn yet determined, trembled as she gathered the nerve to say the words that would irrevocably alter our lives:

"Your dad and I are getting a divorce."

The world spun around me in a blur, sinking inward as time stood still.

Johnathan looked at Mom and uttered, "You are going to hell for this."

Those words cut deep. They hit me then, and they still hit now. I had the understanding in my body of why he said that, but my brain wouldn't allow me to access it. A wall had slammed shut within me, burying that understanding beneath layers of confusion and hurt.

The only emotions I could understand were Mom's: a contagious, crushing sadness that sucked out life energy. My mind was flooded and only able to echo her pain. I was desperate to comfort her. Later on, she blamed the divorce on Dad cheating while he was out on the road. I was nine and not sure what to believe.

Things were bad and getting worse fast, and this was the first acknowledgment from Mom that life was now different

.

CHAPTER FIVE:

The Fork in the Road

Paul started coming more frequently, unbothered by the turmoil he was causing. He was only interested in how to feel good. When we dared to voice our displeasure, his temper flared, shouting at and berating us in our own home, in front of our mother.

Johnathan couldn't stand to be bullied any longer. He saw Mom throwing her life away. He saw her throwing *our* life away.

Despite the reasonable reaction, his concerns were dismissed as the outbursts of an "angry teenager" by both Mom and some of our extended family. That type of gaslighting erodes the trust in your own instincts and perception of reality, a burden that can feel impossible to undo.

On my ninth birthday, April 24th, 2002, Mom and Paul were up to their usual indulgence when Johnathan had enough. He spoke up for not only himself, but his younger brothers, and not only to his mother, but to this strange man that was in our home.

Paul screamed at him in his face, trying to intimidate and assert dominance through size. He didn't care if what he was doing was right, he simply recognized that he could beat this child in a fight if it came down to it.

That pushed Johnathan over the edge and he went to the kitchen and grabbed a knife to protect himself.

For that moment, the dynamic had changed. Despite the cacophony of screaming, we were finally heard.

Johnathan called the police, but was ultimately the one arrested and taken away, as I cried out in horror at what I was witnessing. Paul remained in our home, an unbearably repulsive and infuriating sight after the last few months of torment.

I desperately wanted to talk some sense into her, but in that moment, Mom picked her side and solidified our fate. That was the fork in the road and she chose her new fling over her first-born child.

To be so brazenly uncaring to her children during their adolescence, and to turn her back on her son, is hard to come to terms with now that I'm an adult, especially someone I'd considered to be such a great mother.

If I had my adult mind, this story would have ended there. We would have found anywhere else to go. But not only was Mom the person I was closest to on Earth, she was also the boss. Instead, my brain began shutting down in a frantic attempt at self-preservation.

In the city newspaper's Matters of Record section, it was written as:

April 24 - A juvenile was arrested for aggravated assault, criminal damage, and disorderly conduct against Patricia X. XXXXX & Paul X. XXXXX. There was $50 damage to a wooden door at 240 Walnut.

The mention of the $50 damage to the door repulses me, but also demonstrates their petty nature. Desperate to show they are in the right.

Appearing in the paper for that was a black mark on Johnathan, even without his name. The people who mattered knew exactly who the juvenile in question was. One month earlier, a different name had appeared in the paper.

March 12 - Paul XXXXX was arrested for aggravated battery and disorderly conduct against XXXX X. XXXXXXXX at 619 W. Ninth.

Johnathan was led out by the police that night and never returned to 240 Walnut. He bounced around from Grandma's, to our aunt and uncle in the neighboring town, and back to Grandma's.

Paul not only stayed that night, but he doubled down and planted himself there continuously, almost to prove a point. He was there when we tried to go to sleep. He was there in the morning, awake from the night before, and he would be there after school.

Josh stayed, caught between the naivety of youth and the awareness that comes with age, confused and upset, but not fully able to comprehend why. From what he has told me later in life, he shut down also, as Mom had her attention on us after Johnathan left.

Our brains were not developed enough to have the capacity to take in what was going on and respond clearly, especially with the manipulation we were experiencing. On the rare occasion we did respond, it didn't come out right. On another loud weeknight of parties, Josh walked out there with the intention of asking them to turn down the music so we could sleep, but instead all that came out was, "I don't care!" He froze up and returned to his room.

I don't remember much else from this specific period except those parties. Sitting in a dark room, trying to ease my troubled mind, would have been hard enough on its own with Johnathan leaving. But with constant partying and bad characters coming in and out of the house, it was brain-scrambling.

Later in life, I learned that behind the scenes, some of my aunts and uncles staged an intervention with Mom that failed. Her brother refused to go without his gun, unsure of what he might encounter.

We had ideas about what was going on, but we were constantly lied to, manipulated, and kept in the dark, left to question our own sanity.

Life didn't make sense at that point. The eight years I'd lived before that did not prepare me for what was happening and the choice I was about to be faced with.

Mom didn't know it yet, but Johnathan and Josh would be leaving with Dad after the school year. Even though she was the one who was forcing them out, I knew that she would be devastated.

If they were both leaving and then I left too, she would have nothing, I thought. I pictured her as I'd seen her so many times, sitting at the edge of her bed, face buried in her hands, shoulders shaking with each sob, while the soft sound of *Butterfly Kisses*, a haunting echo from her dad's funeral, played in the background.

The same cry I would attempt to comfort in the middle of the night after her and Paul got into a fight. It's a tormented cry, full of hopelessness. It's crippling to see your mother cry like that at nine years old. It's an image that is seared into my mind and burned into my heart, easy to access whether I want to or not. I didn't just hear it—I absorbed it as my own.

Despite her ripping our family apart, it hurt to see her in that state. I worried that I'd only be adding to the grief. I was sure the guilt would haunt me forever and that I'd keep replaying it, wishing I hadn't left her.

I wasn't happy with what was happening. I was scared and confused. I desperately didn't want to lose my brothers, but I also couldn't conceive of it. They had always been there. I knew that life at 240 Walnut was bad and about to get worse once they left, but my choice was clear. I don't remember any specific conversations, but I knew that my dad and brothers wouldn't approve of the decision, but I had made up my mind.

The thing that made me stay was to try and take care of Mom, but that wasn't the only reason. Goodland was all I had ever known and I was a little kid, scared to leave. Most of all, I was grasping on to the last bit of the old life I had left.

After the last day of school in May 2002, Johnathan and Josh left Goodland. I didn't get to say goodbye. It all happened so fast. Suddenly, they were gone.

I understand now that was the only way they could have made it out from Mom. For their sake, I'm glad they left, even if it cut deep and left a festering wound to not have them there. But the wound that got attention was Mom's.

Her and I came home together and learned they were gone. That day was one of the angriest I'd ever seen her. My pain of losing them was compounded by the heartache radiating from her, twisted and distorted by her all-encompassing wrath, without concern for the one who stayed. She couldn't have been more furious that day, not only at Dad, but with her own boys too. Mom could become irate before substances came into the picture, but once they were combined, she was a force to be reckoned with.

Yes, in hindsight, any reasonable adult would have seen this coming, and though it was a result of her own actions, she still felt the pain of a mom who lost her kids.

Mom and Paul called the cops on my dad for kidnapping Johnathan and Josh, declaring that the war had just started as they plotted their revenge. My brothers were no longer there for the first time in my life. The comforting love from my mom was fading away, too.

CHAPTER SIX

Isolation

Those first few months after my dad and brothers left were the most vile stretch in my life. The voicemails that I heard Mom and Paul leave for my dad were horrific, indicating violence was coming.

In their minds, my dad had kidnapped and indoctrinated the boys, or "poisoned their minds," as they called it. With that belief, they were morally superior and justified to do anything.

The baseline was yelling death threats into the phone. Not hollow ones, but specific ones with planned out destinations, accomplices, and weaponry that Paul would discuss when he hung up the phone, making sure I was in earshot. Plans like coming to find Johnathan and Josh and taking them back by force and disposing of my dad in the process.

There was a certain mania to them, not only anger, but fury stripped of reason. They had crossed into a place where fantasy and reality blurred. To them, bloodshed was a reasonable next step.

Dad did anything but surrender to those threats. He returned one of their messages with a voicemail of his own, declaring that if they tried it, he would FedEx Paul's head back to my mom.

Those hate-filled days turned into a manic party at night, then into a zombie-filled wasteland at the witching hour. When I needed her most, Mom was busy blacking out in the living room with anyone corrupt enough to participate. I lost both of my brothers, my dad, and, effectively, my mom in one fell swoop.

My room was extra empty.

I couldn't even pick up the phone and call them. Mom certainly wouldn't let me communicate with them, with Dad poisoning their minds and all. Her twisted reality was that Johnathan and Dad's accusations were all made up. They barely drank and they *definitely* weren't doing any drugs.

Beyond the boys leaving, the school year had ended, and I was without any friends. I was isolated. In the rare few moments where I found courage and told Mom some of my feelings, I was met with blinding rage, accusations, and insults.

I spent nearly every waking hour in that room. Days bled into nights, then into days again. I memorized every crack in the ceiling, every scuff on the wall. Time warped and lost meaning. It was just me, alone with thoughts that didn't let up.

On countless nights, I'd be trapped in my room during these parties. In the wee hours of the morning, drowning in it and desperate for sleep, I would unleash a primal howl into my pillow, crying as hard as a person can cry, pleading for it to all be over soon.

I tried to make sense of my new reality, but nothing added up.

One day, we were a full family. Next thing I knew, everyone was gone. I would lie in bed at night running over everything that had happened, everything that led up, trying to figure out what I did wrong, why nobody was coming back.

I was a sensitive young boy whose life had fallen apart.

I had nothing left. The mom I had was gone. I had no brothers. No dad. Not a person in the world that I could talk to about all of this.

It was 2002. I had no phone to mindlessly scroll through. I didn't have a TV to turn on and distract myself. I was face to face with my exploding emotions and trauma. It was more than I could process. My brain was buckling under the weight of everything hitting me at once.

The partying was unrelenting, oftentimes lasting all through the night. It came to a point where the overload became too much. I was frantic to the point I worried my heart might short-circuit.

I didn't know how to make myself feel better in the midst of mania, so sometimes I would punch myself in the face, over and over, desperate to find a release from my emotional avalanche, but all I got was dizzy.

I'd hyperventilate to the edge of blackout, choking on my own sobs, the room spinning out of control.

When it was over, I'd lie there in a heap. Heart fluttering. Body trembling. Sweat soaked through my shirt. Eyes swollen shut.

CHAPTER SEVEN:

Man of the House

My dad was the epitome of cool in my eyes. I loved pointing him out as my dad. Same with my brothers.

And Mom traded them for a person I could not have wanted to be associated with any less. I was ashamed to be connected to him. If there was ever an opposite of my dad, it was Paul.

She catered to Paul's every wish, refilling his plate and fetching beers before he had to ask. He was rarely decent enough to say thank you. He was on our couch and never seemed to find a reason to stand up.

Paul had no shame. Take, for example, how he now wore the shoes Dad had to leave behind while rescuing his children. The same shoes he would shoot basketball with us in. The same shoes that had sat by the back door in the laundry room for as long as I could remember were now on the feet of the person I hated most in the world.

Months had now passed, and the 4th of July arrived. For once, Paul was out of the house during the day. I sat on the couch, instead of my room, and got lost in drawing. It was a warm blanket of comfort I hadn't had in a while to see the sun shine through the windows down onto the carpet. The quiet was precious. Back then, my obsession was drawing world-class tour buses—double-deckers, some with swimming pools, almost all with multiple TVs. I loved sketching the compartments, picturing what I'd fill them with, and imagining what life inside them might look like.

That notebook has somehow survived all these years, a rare memento from that time.

To nobody's surprise, that night, there was a party at 240 Walnut. There was a flicker of excitement when I recognized someone from my old life, my brother's friend Aaron who came with his mother.

I wandered through my own home that night and didn't recognize most of the people. There was plenty of booze flowing and Mom's bedroom door was closed with clear directions for me to stay away.

Later on into the night, an argument between Aaron's mom and Paul's friend became physical and Aaron jumped in to fight the adult and protect his mother.

After the fight was broken up and before the police arrived, Paul got on his soapbox, ranting at the top of his lungs: "If anyone's throwing a punch in this house, it's gonna be me."

I don't know who called the cops, but I remember feeling bothered that Paul was the one talking to them when they arrived, like *he* was the man of the house.

Once again the child, this time Aaron, was taken away in handcuffs, leaving the drunken fiends to party in peace.

As the man of the house, Paul also made sure to expand my vocabulary.

During one of the good nights when Paul managed to leave 240 Walnut, Mom and I played a game of mad libs out of an activity book at night before I went to bed. It was the kind of calm bonding that I desperately needed. But I knew I was in the eye of the storm.

She tucked me in that night the way she used to, and the sheets in my bed felt amazing. Warm, clean, and finally still, I sank into them and for a moment, let go of everything I'd been holding all day.

Later that night, I woke up to the sounds of one of the worst fights they had yet. The anger was blistering and becoming out of control. I wasn't only in danger myself. Mom was too. Paul continued stomping around screaming about the violence he could unleash on not only her, but me as well.

His voice cut through the pounding music. And so did Mom's. She met him head-on. Not flinching. Not giving an inch.

"This is exactly why your kids left you and your brothers won't have anything to do with you. You're fucking crazy. Nobody loves you! We're all waiting for you to die," Paul said, throwing in a callous laugh at the end.

"You are so fucking cruel," she responded.

"At least I've been a parent to my kids," she said, finding her fire again.

"I ought to bust your fucking lip," he replied.

"Do you realize what I could do to you? You and your fucking son," he growled, his voice thick with disgust and hatred. Then he went quiet, and now the silence seemed worse.

The shouting spiraled, sharper and faster, until it peaked in one brutal sound. A sickening thud. Dead weight and bone hitting the carpet. Then nothing again.

Silence, sudden and total.

She didn't say another word that night.

My stomach turned and I froze in place. Every part of me locked up. I didn't move, didn't breathe.

I wanted to run to her to see if she was okay, but I couldn't. I laid there and ate it. And hoped she was still breathing.

I didn't witness Paul punch Mom, but I heard and saw the results when she couldn't hide it. She had an answer for everything. Her black eye? A walk into a door, she'd claim. The bruises on the side of her face and forehead? Just a fall down the stairs.

I was young enough that I hadn't heard those excuses before. In my heart I knew they weren't true, but I wanted so desperately to believe her.

That next morning, I found the Mad Libs book on the counter. There was a word scribbled on the outside cover that wasn't there the night before. I wanted it to be a sweet note from Mom, maybe letting me know she was okay after last night. Scratched in deeply with the pen one word stuck out above all the rest, the word "cunt."

That was the first time I'd encountered that word. A cold dread settled over me, wondering what would happen when Paul woke up.

CHAPTER EIGHT

Unraveling

I don't remember seeing Paul that next day. Last night must have been a turning point, because he was gone.

In the days after he became absent, a new male figure emerged. I'll call him Gary.

Mom sensed my hesitation about another strange man coming into the house and went on about how she knew him from when they were younger, basically trying to convey that this wasn't a person from her new life.

There was a certain sliminess that I couldn't put my finger on with Gary. He smiled, but it didn't quite reach his eyes. It was thin and unconvincing.

I wasn't sure if I didn't trust him because he was another new person, or because my gut was warning me.

The partying didn't stop, but it was much less chaotic than with Paul. Gary was seemingly respectful to Mom, and generally treated me well, even throwing football with me in the yard one afternoon. Part of me wondered if I was being too quick to judge, considering that I might have had the wrong first impression.

That weekend, Gary ended up staying overnight.

When I woke up the next morning, I had finally caught my breath after what felt like a night spent underwater. My underwear were off of me and nowhere to be found. I was upside down in my bed. My limbs were heavy and slow to respond, as if my body hadn't caught up to the fact that I was awake.

I was alone, but I was also embarrassed.

My sense of time was off and I couldn't remember anything from the night before. A nauseating feeling was flooding my system. I wasn't sure if it was me or the world that had shifted.

When I came out of my room that day, Gary was already gone. His stay had abruptly ended and he disappeared into the background of Goodland's many unsavory characters, but always seeming to keep his distance.

I never considered telling Mom. Or anyone else.

It settled into that same hidden corner of my heart where no one else got to see. Where it festered. Quiet, but constant. It didn't bellow for my attention. It sat there, shaping the way I experienced life, whether I realized it or not.

I wish I could say definitively, but I don't know what happened that night.

The line between truth and lies was completely blurred, leaving me more than confused, because so much of what was going on was behind closed doors. My instincts about what was going on were strong, but I was passionately lied to over and over again.

I suspected there was more than just alcohol involved, but I hadn't seen it with my own eyes.

As quickly as Gary left, Paul was back. This time, things only escalated when he returned. There were fewer people coming over, but the two of them partied harder than ever.

They would be drinking beer when I woke up, throughout the day, then switching to their favorite liquor at night. I often woke up to the familiar hiss and pop of a can opening.

The confusion of everything was getting to me. I was trapped in that house with the two people tearing it apart. Their moods swung without warning, and it was impossible to know what version of them I would get. I had no one to ask, no one to run to. Just the noise and the tension.

After driving home from a particularly drunken night at the bowling alley, Paul sat out in our Suburban parked in the driveway, the last big purchase of the previous marriage, blasting "Momma I'm Coming Home" by Ozzy Osbourne as loud as possible. Mom was crying, stomping in and out of the house, her voice ripping through the air at him.

Mom called on me, asking for my help getting Paul from the car to inside the house because he was too intoxicated to walk. We were on either side of him, as he swayed back and forth against us, incoherent. As the two of us walked him up the short staircase in front of the house, he lurched towards my side and his weight was too much for a nine-year-old. I couldn't hold him and he fell through the railing and directly into the flower bed.

The same flower bed that Mom and Dad put so much love and care into. Only to be destroyed by someone Mom let in. Someone so self-absorbed that he didn't care to see the path of destruction left in his wake.

Paul passed out immediately in the flower bed. There was no way we were getting him up, so he stayed out there for the night.

The next day nobody addressed what happened. The same cycle continued without missing a beat.

If you couldn't tell, Mom and Paul had an insatiable appetite for partying. Days continued to consist of the two getting drunk and blasting music, before devolving into a bitter argument at night. They would scream at each other at the top of their lungs and it was often a contest of who could go lower before a glass got thrown or a fist went through drywall.

Not only was I too small and scared to do anything, but both of them had previously accused me of bad intentions when I worked up the fortitude to try and help. Mom would turn the rage and hate towards me, reminding me that *she* was the mom.

She would ask, "What do you think, I'm fucking stupid?"

I was a little boy trying in earnest to help his mom stop crying and screaming when a psychotic man was in our house saying the nastiest things I had ever heard in my life about her. Things a little kid shouldn't ever hear about his mother. He called her a worthless nasty whore, crackhead bitch, stupid cunt. He loved to taunt her about the mistakes she was making in life and tell her nobody cared about her. He would insult and threaten her in every way imaginable, at the top of his lungs, making sure I could hear everything he was saying.

One night, things escalated further and Paul went on a rampage. From my room, I heard him wail as if he'd lost all touch with reality. He stomped around the house breaking glass and throwing furniture, a kitchen chair and side table as I later discovered.

Mom yelped, I'm not sure if it was out of fear or pain, but her signature defiance was gone. She was no longer responding to Paul's insults. I heard her take shelter in her room, closing the door behind her. He stomped towards us and stood in the hallway between our doors.

"I'm done. I'm getting my fucking gas can, and I'm gonna burn this motherfucker to the ground," Paul erupted.

Mom responded with a sobering, "Paul, please."

I'd heard her upset before, but this was different. I could hear the panic in her voice. A tremble I'd never heard before. Her pleas only increased his already boiling rage.

Paul responded, "You think I'm fucking kidding?" and slammed his fist against her door.

His voice dropped, eerily calm. "Both of you are going to die tonight."

The blood drained from my face. I'd heard many threats between the two of them, but the terror I had was primal, a deep, instinctive knowledge that the threat was real, and immediate.

I didn't want it to be true. I hoped with all my being that he was bluffing and that he and Mom would make up.

Her sobs were easy to hear from down the hall. She muttered to herself, asking "Why?", seemingly already accepting her fate.

The screen door screeched as I heard Paul walk outside. Without a thought, I ran out of my bedroom to close and lock the front door.

Through the front window, I watched Paul stagger toward his truck, his actions fueled by something more than anger. He yanked a gas can from the bed and disappeared into the backyard.

When I got eyes on him again, he was under the yellow glow of the porch light, pouring gasoline against the house. The liquid hit the walls in splashes, the harsh scent creeping inside. Paul was muttering to himself, the words lost in a mess of incoherence. The horror of it all didn't register at first. But when it did, it was all at once. He wasn't bluffing. He was really going to do it.

I turned to walk toward Mom's room as time began to slow. The hallway stretched long and endless, her door pulling farther and farther away. I wanted to wake up, furious at the reality that I couldn't. It wasn't only my heart sinking, it was everything inside me. My veins were rubber bands stretched too far and on the verge of snapping.

My body took control in a panic, moving before my mind could catch up. I ran to Mom's room to find her sitting on her bed crying.

"Mom! What are we gonna do?" I yelled out.

But she didn't answer. She didn't even glance at me.

I wanted to shake her and ask, "Why are you letting this happen?"

But something deeper ached. I was gutted at the sight of her. She looked small and folded into herself. It was clear she had already given up. I was on my own. There was no adult to step in, no one to fix this. If I didn't act fast, we were both going to die. The anxiety inside me sharpened and my adrenaline surged.

In a last-ditch desperation, I grabbed her phone and dialed 911 and ran to the kitchen and the back window.

Passivity was no longer an option.

With all my might and muster, I conjured my high-pitched, high-powered shriek, and I screamed like my life depended on it.

"I'm calling the cops! I'm calling the cops! I'm calling the cops!"

Paul froze.

Even through the glass, I saw it. A flicker of hesitation.

Cops meant consequences. He had a record. They knew him. And with whatever he had on him, he couldn't risk it.

Mom stomped into the kitchen, her face twisting with fury and wet with tears. She was out of her hole.

"Hang up the phone!" she said through gritted teeth.

I could feel the anger emanating off her. I had no choice. My hands shook as I ended the call before it ever started.

But the damage was already done. I had crossed Paul.

He stood there for another second, his breath heavy, and turned and disappeared to the side of the house.

The sound of his pickup rumbled and then roared as he left 240 Walnut.

CHAPTER NINE

The Return

Paul returned the next day without shame. Mom acted like we were the ones who had crossed the line. She treated him as if he were royalty, waiting on him hand and foot, bringing him food and drinks without prompt.

Around this time, I realized that we were becoming very poor. I remember watching Mom count wadded up dollar bills and coins to see if there was enough to get cigarettes or gas to go to the store. If we could pay for everything in the cart at the grocery store without putting anything back, it was a small miracle. She didn't have a credit card, so we either had the money or we didn't. More often than not, we didn't.

At the end of the summer, school supply shopping that year seemed like my fault, as if it was superfluous. The years of getting new shoes to start the school year were only a memory. Soon enough, I'd become the sympathy donation spot for the extended family. I greatly appreciated it, but it just confirmed what I already believed—I was lesser.

Later that year in school, we were asked to bring non-perishables to school to help the needy for the holidays. It was a great time for me not sitting in the classroom and rather packing things up in the hallway, helping out those in need. The confusion in my heart and my brain when I saw one of those same boxes in my living room later that week was heavy.

I wasn't resentful about becoming poor, or upset about it. Despite all that had happened, I was under the impression that Mom and I were as close as two people could be. I was there with her to make life a little better, because of how much she had told me she loved me. In my heart, I wanted to believe that we were poor because of the situation we were in, but now I realize that wasn't as much the case. We didn't have to be as poor as we were.

When my parents were together, Mom had taken care of the accounting while Dad worked. He had a solid job and money coming in, but Dad received none of the savings that had been built up over the years in the divorce. That was gone.

I didn't know it yet, but Mom had no longer been making mortgage payments and the bank would soon be foreclosing on the house. I'd watch Mom doing the math on the backside of an envelope, trying to figure out how we were going to make ends meet. She picked up a job at the bowling alley. And then another at a local cafe. Paul chose not to work for now.

This was only the beginning of the stress that poverty would bring into my life.

Lucky for Mom and Paul, a divorce hearing was imminent, with a possibility of regaining custody of Johnathan and Josh, with a large child support check likely to follow.

Luckily for me, Dad and my brothers would be returning to Goodland for the divorce hearing. It had only been a few months after they had left, but to me, it might as well have been forever.

After they'd left, the three traveled the country and lived out of hotel rooms during the summer while Dad worked. He later landed a job in Issaquah, Washington, and took the family there to settle down.

Paul taunted me, ensuring their return wouldn't be a pleasant experience. He laughed wildly, explaining over and over how he was going to fight my dad on the courthouse lawn, talking through all of the combinations of punches he would throw, eventually leading to a curb stomp.

I was just excited to see my family.

Mom, a mess of anticipation and despair, awaited the reunion with her boys. Somewhere down deep in her was the mom that we grew up with and she was devastated. She was dying to see them, but also knew she faced another dreaded goodbye.

When that day finally came, Mom and I drove out to a parking lot on Highway 24 to meet them.

The emotions that we all had tried to bury bubbled up to the surface.

Josh and Johnathan's scowls spoke volumes. They weren't happy to be back. They were living in her consequences as much as I was. Their mom had kicked them out, forcing a move across the country. Again, Dad had landed a stable job, but all the money he'd saved was gone, so he was truly starting with nothing.

When we met that day, all Mom wanted was to hug her boys. And she did, but they were understandably reluctant. The love she was so desperate to show that day was ripped from them, by her, a few months before. Even so, I wanted them to forgive her. I knew how much it would mean to her.

Mom was a special kind of sad that day. The part of her that wanted to be the old great mom that she was before was drowned in substances, but it was still there. It hurt her to see her boys and have them not show her love, though they showed her more love than she deserved at the time. The fact that they took the meeting was generous enough.

Her emotional level would have been justified if not for her actions, but that didn't stop me from feeling her pain.

Seeing my brothers after such a long absence was hard to make sense of. Our interactions used to be so seamless, but now I was questioning how to speak to them. My unconvincing "sup," a new bit of slang that I'd picked up since they'd left, was met with a scoff from Josh.

Both of the boys now towered over Mom. They had grown their hair out and wore tighter fitting clothes with band logos that I wasn't familiar with. Not through any fault of their own, but a sense of unfamiliarity had settled in between us.

Nobody really had the appetite to say much other than Mom. The wounds were too raw for casual conversation. It was quiet between us boys because we didn't have the space or capacity to *actually* talk to each other. We drove around Goodland and out into the country and posed for horribly awkward photos, as Mom tried desperately to pretend that everything was normal.

Josh took my red, white, and blue skateboarding armband that I was wearing and put it on his forearm. I loved that little armband, but I wanted to believe that he took it to have a connection to his old life, and maybe even to me.

After the painful meeting was done, we boys went and stayed with Dad at the hotel. We went and got burgers together, but after traveling all day, they were tired and ready to go to bed.

What happened in the courtroom that next day is largely a mystery to me. I wouldn't learn the details until years later, but the hearing resulted in a child support order requiring Dad to send Mom $1,750 per month. When I found out later in life, I couldn't comprehend it. One of the constant truths of my life was that we had nothing. We were dead broke, constantly teetering on the edge of losing everything. That was true, but it didn't have to be.

Once it was over, Johnathan and Josh left with Dad and I stayed in Goodland with Mom. We returned to 240 Walnut where I was sure Paul was waiting.

CHAPTER TEN

Abandoned

Mercifully, Summer break had ended, offering a temporary escape from the chaos as I entered the fourth grade. There was nobody to confide in. I was too protective of my secrets and too embarrassed to share them. So, I wore a happy face and pretended that my life wasn't falling apart.

After school one afternoon, Mom wasn't there to pick me up. So I walked, nervous about what would be unfolding once I got home that kept her from coming to get me. When I got home, the door was locked. I tried it again, hoping I'd just messed it up the first time, but it didn't budge.

I rushed to the back door. Locked.

Over to the garage door at the rear. That was locked too.

Every window was shut, every latch secure. I circled around to the front door and tried again. I had never realized how solid a door is until I didn't have the keys to get in.

My heart sank, realizing the weight of the situation. The panic set in as I realized that I had no access to a phone, no keys, no transportation. All I could do was wait.

I sat there on the front steps trying my best to stay calm.. Each passing moment stretched out endlessly. The autumn air was crisp, and the distant, muffled noise of my neighbors going about their lives was cutting. I knew I couldn't ask for help.

What was I going to say? How could I explain this without making Mom look bad? If I left and she came back while I was gone, it would have been betrayal.

Maybe I overreacted. She would be home soon, I tried to tell myself.

Eventually, I grabbed my backpack and moved to the backyard. I slipped deeper into madness as the afternoon turned to evening and the evening turned to night.

In that endless stretch of time, my emotions surged uncontrollably. A tsunami of sadness and despair morphed into searing anger, then into bitter regret and paralyzing hopelessness. I was upset to the point of feeling unstable, pacing around, talking to myself, desperate for anything to ease my troubled heart.

It all came rushing in: memories, questions, fears. I became fixated with tunnel-vision on whatever the most overwhelming one was. My arms would tense up, aching to unleash that fury in a desperate punch. I almost wailed, but the sound died in my throat, leaving a pitiful gargle.

The cold seeped into my bones, not only as an external chill, but an existential ache that rooted itself within me, down to the marrow.

At points, I imagined that they were in the house, passed out. Other times I was convinced they were quietly hiding because they didn't want me inside. I imagined the worst scenarios of what had happened to Mom. Like finding her dead on the side of the road after Paul followed through with one of his threats, with no evidence to the contrary to ground me.

The overblown ideas of what might have happened that helped fuel my manic energy started to crumble and were replaced by a crushing sense of exhaustion. I was worn down, raw, and depleted to nothing.

There wasn't anything left to do, so I curled up on the landing and tried to go to sleep.

My mind couldn't make sense of much that night, but one thought was crystal clear as I lay outside: *I badly wanted my mom.* The mom that used to cut our waffles exactly how we liked them. The one that never let us go to sleep without getting tucked in and hearing sweet dreams. I wanted that *so bad.*

That night, the last of my childhood mind gave way. Dried out and carried off like topsoil in the wind, never to be put back where it belonged. Instead of having an unfiltered, honest internal dialogue rich with curiosity, it went mostly blank and silent. The vibrant chatter of my youth, those endless questions and big dreams, had vanished.

The next morning, it was clear Mom wasn't coming home. I weighed my options and quickly realized there was only one, so I grabbed my backpack and walked a half-mile to Grandma's house at 206 Broadway.

Up to this point, we hadn't been all that close. Of course I loved her, she was my grandma, but in the first years of my life she was very much a secondary character to Grandpa. After he died, I saw her a lot less.

I'm not sure what I said to her when I showed up on her doorstep, but I doubt that I had much to say. Without hesitation, she took me in and accepted me with the full love of her heart. I'll never forget the hug she gave me that day. It was strong. It was secure. It was completely loving.

By now, I had been trained to not share what was happening at home. Mom told me that what happens in the house, stays in the house. If that wasn't enough, she and Paul went on and on about how everyone was talking about them behind their backs, conspiring to take them down by whatever means necessary.

Grandma called in and told the school I wouldn't be there that day. She quickly put me at ease, loading me up with sodas and snacks as we sat in her bed and watched daytime television. *The Price is Right, Maury,* and eventually *Days of Our Lives.* The elephant in the room was overshadowed by her infectious laughter. Her unwavering positivity shielded me. Her eyes sent a constant reminder of how much I mattered to her.

The next morning, Grandma was up early to take me to school and by the time I got out of school that day, the kitchen had been restocked with me in mind. She gave me a new shirt and sweats while she washed the clothes I was wearing. A message to me that I was welcome to stay.

Days later, when I got in Grandma's car again after school, she told me that Mom would be coming back to pick me up that night after the two had a private conversation. Deep down, I didn't want to leave the safety, security, and love of Grandma's house, but that part of me was buried, and there was really no choice anyway.

When Mom picked me up, there was no apology. She told me that it was wrong of me to question her. She was an adult after all.

This wouldn't be the only instance of abandonment around this time. Some of the darkest days I struggle to recall were the ones spent locked out of 240 Walnut with no sign of Mom. Then, walking to Grandma's, hoping with everything that she was there, praying I didn't find her door locked, like when she was out of town visiting one of her other kids.

The hopeless feeling of knocking on a door, desperate for a response, still lives inside of me. Even a few seconds innocently locked out triggers that same sinking sensation, a cold dread, as the knob refuses to budge.

After Mom took me back to 240 Walnut that day, their paranoia had reached new highs. Mom sat me down and questioned me about what the family was saying about them or what I had told them about what was happening when she was gone. When I said nothing, she accused me of lying and taking their side.

"You are a bold-faced fucking liar," she seethed.

According to her and Paul, Grandma and the rest of her family were actively plotting against her to take me away.

Mom was no longer the person I'd known growing up, and the change was only accelerating. She had moments of normalcy. Other times, I could speak directly to her and she wouldn't respond at all, or if she did, her responses were off. She was confused, angry, and disconnected, as if part of her wasn't there.

Not knowing what else to believe, I assumed she was very upset or acting differently because of me, or my brothers, or Dad, or Paul.

The explosive episodes that Paul flew into came quicker and with less warning. They would often be because of simple misunderstandings, such as not hearing someone correctly.

I learned to make myself small in all moments, desperate to keep everyone calm. Formulating precisely the right thing to say to keep their moods from tanking. I sacrificed my own thoughts and needs in a desperate attempt to keep everyone from flying off the handle.

I didn't witness Mom or Paul using it directly, but their lives, and mine, bore the unmistakable signs of methamphetamine use. I know this not only from personal experience living with them, but because in moments when Paul wanted to dress Mom down in front of me. He would openly talk about their drug use—like the time they spotted one of her brothers across the campground while they were boldly smoking meth at their site at the Smoky. Or about how Mom was actually upset that particular day because Paul and a friend decided not to share their meth with her. She would be stunned silent, boiling with hate and hurt, not refuting anything, but staring a hole through Paul, silently begging him to stop.

Even without Paul's admissions, the evidence was clear. Looking back, it was mainly the delusions of grandeur. They'd boast about having a deeper understanding of the world, that everyone else was beneath them, living in blissful ignorance. Conversations devolved into rants against family and Mom accusing them all of corruption and conspiring against her.

According to the National Institute on Drug Abuse, "long-term methamphetamine use can cause anxiety, confusion, insomnia, and mood disturbances.

Symptoms of psychosis, such as seeing and/or hearing things that are not there (hallucinations) and deeply believing false stories or ideas (delusions), even when not intoxicated," may also occur. "Heavy drinking and stress have been shown to increase the odds" of these symptoms returning in those with past meth-induced psychosis.

Reading this twenty years later, it makes perfect sense, but as a nine-year-old, I was completely fucking confused.

Some of those same traits can appear with other drugs, but if you have ever been around a meth user, you know there is a very specific type of crazy that comes with it. When you are coming down from any drug, it's unpleasant, so you want to keep consuming to stave it off, but at some point you are going to come back down. As high as you were, you will go equally as low afterwards. With meth in particular, that come down seems particularly bad.

The environment was normally shaky, one of the two ready to snap, but when they were coming down was when things got the scariest and most unpredictable. Trying to reason with them was impossible. The most rational requests would be met with unbelievable levels of fury and screaming, the same as if I'd told them they were pieces of shit. They'd be red-faced, fully immersed in the pool of hate, their voices tearing through the room with raw, unfiltered rage. As Mom used to say, they had "come unglued."

Again at the time, I didn't know what to think. Maybe it was me. Maybe it was the divorce.

Mom also repeatedly told me that I wasn't old enough to understand. She was the mom and if I questioned her, I was implying that she was stupid or calling into question her ability to be a parent. She screamed at me repeatedly, telling me that she would *never* put me in danger.

In my few moments of bravery, I would go to her and let a grain of my true feelings out about how I was feeling. She reacted with a ferocity that could have singed the hair on my arms. She was offended at the entire conversation and

threw lies in my face, frequently claiming that my dad had somehow poisoned my mind.

Or that my grandma had turned me against her. Or worst of all, that I just had some sort of ill will and hatred towards her and was only acting to make her life worse.

I learned to not say anything. Later on, in the rare moments when she would ask, I went involuntarily mute, unable to put together any words at all. It was complete silence, other than my sobs.

Those experiences created a block for me that I have to actively work on overcoming to this day. Not only doubting my feelings, but not even having the ability to access or understand them in the privacy of my own head. I've struggled to understand my feelings in the moments of everyday life and especially in my closest relationships, mostly waiting to be beat down when I'm most vulnerable.

Chapter Eleven

The End of 240 Walnut

One of the moments that has stuck out in my mind was when Mom sat us boys down to tell us that her and Dad were getting a divorce. It was an out-of-body experience where I could feel the future shifting under my feet.

One of the other moments came when Mom sat me down at the kitchen table and told me that we had to leave 240 Walnut and that we would be moving in with Paul.

As unsafe as things had been lately, the fact that 240 Walnut was ours, not Paul's, felt like a small safety net. Now, when the fights blew up, it wouldn't be clear who would be expected to leave. More than that, living there was the last bit of hope I had to hold onto that things might go back to normal.

Sitting quietly in that moment, I was hanging over the edge of a tall building and my grip was slipping. But I had one last chance to hold on. So, I tried. Swallowing my distress and attempting to communicate as clearly as I could, I explained that I *really* didn't want to go.

As coherent as I tried to be, I was completely confused and not able to understand my own feelings. I was respectful when talking to her, but in the privacy of my own head, I hated Paul with every fiber of my being. He never apologized or acknowledged that he had done anything wrong. There were nights I lay awake wishing I were bigger and stronger so I could defend her, or that I were ballsy enough to take it further.

In whatever way I was able to articulate it, it wasn't received well by Mom. She broke down into tears herself.

"I don't want to die alone," she sobbed.

I didn't know how to reply to that.

That's the last memory I have of us living at 240 Walnut.

Leaving there was foundation-breaking. I loved that house. There were three bedrooms on the main level, one downstairs in the basement. We had a front yard and a huge backyard. Looking it up online today, it's listed at around 1,000 square feet.

It was everything I could have ever wanted as a kid. Not only had I made almost all of my core memories there, my memories started there.

Despite my heartache, we moved from 240 Walnut to 619 W 9th Street, a 576-square-foot white house on the opposite end of Goodland. There was no room for our furniture and other belongings, as Paul elected to get his stuff out of storage and move it in. All of our possessions except our clothes and my bed went into storage, a lot of which I never saw again.

The horrific way that Paul made me feel was now inescapable. It was in the walls, the furniture, and definitely his utensils. Those objects no longer held the memories I'd made with my family, they were now unsettling and unfamiliar.

Even before the divorce, I had reservations about using other people's glasses and silverware. I don't trust basically anyone to do the dishes correctly and not leave germs or food behind. I was nauseated to my core when I had to use his silverware. I learned to eat without touching the fork to my mouth, which I still do to this day out of habit.

Moving to a smaller and, frankly, shittier house wouldn't have bugged me if it were just me and Mom. We could have banded together and helped each other.

That was what I hoped would happen when I decided to stay behind when my brothers left. But I didn't feel comfortable at 619 W 9th Street, not for a second.

The first night I had to stay there was Christmas Eve 2004.

In the years prior to things falling apart, Christmas could not have been a bigger deal to me. Aside from the presents, the Butts family would travel from as far as eastern Kansas to come together and Dad would come home for a longer period than his usual few days.

The Butts family gathered once again at 206 Broadway, carrying on the tradition from years past. But after I'd sought refuge at Grandma's house that day back in the fall, Mom had cut off contact with her and anyone else in the family and refused to attend the holiday get-together.

Much to my dismay, I had to fight to be allowed to go. And even then, I showed up late. Mom and Paul had insisted that we would be going to church with his parents that night.

Mom wasn't religious and Paul seemed as far from God as anyone I'd ever met, but apparently it was important that we went that night. With all of the actions I had witnessed in the last year or so, I couldn't believe they would be stepping into a church.

I've noticed that when you are doing drugs and hiding it, the illusions you try and get over on people are really important. Attending church on Christmas Eve strengthened their position in the ongoing battle for perceived virtue.

Sitting at that church wasn't only miserable because it was all so forced and faked by the three of us. It was also miserable because I was a kid wanting to open presents and spend time with some of my favorite family members: Grandma, Uncle Troy, and my cousins Summer and Tim. Christmas with them was all that I had to look forward to for the foreseeable future.

When I did finally get to Butts celebration, it was all that I wanted it to be. I was with people I was comfortable with in a safe place, with no worries of sudden rage, malice, or chaos.

My cousin Summer gifted me a Video Now player, a new handheld video device. Summer and I had shared a close bond from when I was a baby. She was as all-American as they come—sweet as can be, truly salt of the earth, with natural blonde hair, gunmetal blue eyes, and a bright, welcoming smile.

She visited us often in the years prior to the divorce, and she and my mom seemed to get along effortlessly. She'd let me sit on her lap and steer her car on the way home after taking us out for a treat. She tells me now about how sad I looked whenever she had to leave, staring at her from the screen door.

In the middle of the celebration, despite showing up late, Mom called Grandma's house and said it was time for me to come home. I held the phone and talked, noticing a hush over the room and a lot of eyes on me.

When I asked Summer to take me to 619 W 9th Street was when the Butts family learned that we had moved in with Paul. The way Mom eagerly grilled me about their reaction when I got back led me to believe that it wasn't an accident I was positioned to break the news. When I told them, their reactions were masked. It was obvious they had strong feelings, but they didn't know what to say to me.

As we loaded in the car and pulled away, the realization that I really had to return to Paul's house to sleep was coming down on me.

The hug that I gave Summer when she dropped me off would have lasted forever in a perfect world. I wouldn't have had to go in that house and I could stay with her where life still made sense.

But that hug did end.

Summer could tell how depressed I was and told me to let her know if I needed anything. It was a nice sentiment, but reaffirmed the situation I was in. I did need help, desperately, but I couldn't tell her. I couldn't tell anyone. I didn't know the words. And even if I did, I was also so loyal to Mom that telling someone about her hard times was betrayal.

When I walked up to the door, I didn't know whether to knock or go inside. This had never been a question before. But now everything felt different. My hand hovered in the air, caught between reaching for the knob and knocking.

It was a gamble either way. Walking right in might put them off, but knocking might too.

I knocked, and Mom scoffed that I wasn't treating it as my own home. I'd picked wrong.

Aside from that, the mood wasn't great anyway. She was only interested in what her family was saying about her and I couldn't understand why. Now, I see the paranoia. Aside from the drugs, knowing that you are in the wrong, knowing you can see the sadness and hurt on my face, and knowing that your family can see that too must have been overwhelming.

The setting had changed, but the scene was the same. Their music was loud, cigarette smoke filled the room, and the empty beer cans were stacking up. I walked into my new room and sat on the bed, unfamiliar, and its surface uninviting.

The music got louder and an argument broke out between Mom and Paul.

I decided to try out my new Video Now player to drown out the noise. I put on the plastic over-the-ear headphones and watched the "Band Geeks" episode of SpongeBob.

The small distraction was nice. SpongeBob brought a feeling of comfort and normalcy. But their partying was too loud to drown out, so I gave up and just decided to try and sleep. As I lay there, the weight of the situation pressed down on me. Things had finally gone far enough from normal that I didn't see a way back.

After a restless few hours of tossing and turning, running a mile with the thoughts in my mind, desperate for sleep, and racked with tears, I decided to act.

I thought that if I went out there, pleaded as nicely as anyone ever had and explained myself well enough, maybe they would see where I was coming from and consider quieting down. My goal was to make myself small enough in the situation that they couldn't possibly have any reason to get mad at me.

After working up the nerve, I stepped out of my room and walked a few steps to the living room and explained myself as eloquently as I could.

"I'm sorry for even asking, but since it's so late, do you think you maybe could be a little bit more quiet?"

Paul snapped his head to look at me. He stood up to square up with me, like I had challenged him.

"Are you fucking kidding me? You aren't gonna tell me what to do in my own fucking house. Who the fuck do you think you are?"

He stepped toward me, shaking, then turned and stormed through the house, slamming doors and cabinets, shouting, "If you think you're a man, I'll start treating you like one."

I ran back to that unfamiliar room that I hated being in and fell into tears.

Mom not only didn't stick up for me, but she didn't come to check on me either.

After that night, I was changed. My spirit was defeated. It was clearly not a fluke that when I expressed my feelings, I was met with searing anger from the adults around me. If I wanted any hope of staying out of harm's way, I would shut up and take it.

After that, my emotions were hidden, until they burst out of me uncontrollably and unintelligibly.

In the present day, I struggle to grasp my true emotions and find the ability to express them. Especially in my late twenties, strong emotions would bubble up and I wouldn't know why I was horribly depressed, why I was angry, or what I was even feeling. I would get caught down in a hole for hours and, on occasion, disappear into it for days.

Back at 619 W 9th, I had no physical escape, so I started creating one in my head. In my mind, I was no longer a broken 9-year-old boy living his nightmare, I was a professional wrestler, winning championships and dating the top female wrestlers, or whatever other wrestling-adjacent celebrities I happened to know about.

I wasn't riding my bicycle, I was riding a motorcycle, not in Goodland, but I was in Washington, living near Dad and my brothers. Or I was the president, escorted around by the secret service. I was an army special agent. Not just for the time I was playing outside. These fantasies occupied my internal dialogue for long periods.

I'd envision what life would be like if things were different, what situations I would be in. Imagining the experience of returning home to Goodland when I was famous and had security to protect me. They were detailed stories only I knew, stretching on for months at a time. When I would lay down to go to sleep, my attention went to that world instead of the one I was living in. It didn't work all the time, but any break I could get, I would take.

Sometimes, I was certain my life had to be a prank. I waited for cameras to appear and reveal it was all just a sick joke.

CHAPTER TWELVE

Escape to El Dorado

Living at 619 W 9th Street was an uncomfortable blur. There aren't many details that I recall from day-to-day life. Everything I had known—the walls that held my memories, every possession I had for the previous nine years—had been stripped away, leaving me blank.

After school one day, Mom let me know she would be dropping me off at Grandma's for the weekend because she and Paul were going out of town. She said they would come get me in a few days.

Staying at Grandma's was not a problem at all for me. In fact, it felt like coming up for air. But when she failed to return on Monday and after a week passed without any way to reach her, I couldn't take it anymore, and I broke down.

I told Grandma a sliver of what was going on and how stressed I was. She held me and listened, letting me know I was with her now. She didn't pry for information, she just sat and loved me.

My Uncle Troy called Grandma every day to check on her. Once I noticed this routine, I would rush to pick up the phone, savoring any chance I had to talk to him. Troy was unbelievably charismatic and as sweet as they come. His raunchy humor was exactly the kind of thing a young boy would latch onto. And I did.

Decades before this, he had fallen out of a cherry tree and broken his neck. He became paralyzed from the waist down with minimal movement in his arms and hands. His wife Pam became his full-time caretaker as they raised their son, Tim.

After Grandpa died, Troy shone as the light of the family. Unlike most of the other members of the family, he didn't harbor grudges and regularly put effort into communicating with his brothers and sister. In fact, he often brought disgruntled parties together, mainly because of how much they wanted to be around him.

When I got sick years prior to this and had to take breathing treatments, I would cry and refuse to do them unless Troy was on the phone talking me through it. He brought that much joy and comfort to me.

The call from Troy came in right on cue, around four in the afternoon. I picked up the phone and made small talk with him before handing the phone to Grandma. After their conversation, he requested to talk to me again.

Verbally, we circled each other like two wrestlers, and when Troy saw his moment, he went for the takedown. He told me he'd heard about some of what had been going on with my mom and wanted to let me know that I could talk about it with him.

In a moment of divine clarity, I told him I was on the verge of a nervous breakdown. I don't know how, or if I really knew what that meant—I'd probably overheard it from Mom or Grandma—but I think I was right on the money.

Without hesitation, Troy offered for me to come live with him and Pam in El Dorado, 300 miles southeast of Goodland. It wasn't lost on me then, and it's certainly not lost on me today, how much he was putting himself out there. Not only was he taking on the burden of another child living with him while on a fixed income, but Mom had already threatened legal action against Grandma if she didn't give me back after she'd disappeared the first time.

Troy didn't flinch.

Recently, I learned that Grandma went to the prosecuting attorney in Goodland and asked that Pam and Troy not be charged if they took me. I also learned that multiple members of my family had called Child Protective Services on Mom before this.

Nothing had come of those inquiries. After I was told that, I remembered fancier looking adults than my teachers pulling me out of class to talk. They posed general probing questions about my home life, but I was trained well, and I told them everything was fine. It didn't seem unusual. I assumed everyone was going to have to do it, similar to vision or hearing tests. These meetings happened on multiple occasions over the years, but I wasn't able to be honest with myself about what was happening, so they had no chance of getting anything out of me.

I was overwhelmed with fear, but Troy worked his comforting magic, and I agreed to come live with him for a little while, while Mom got back on her feet.

The thought of making my first move against her buried me in a wave of terror. My body hesitated, but some deeper survival instinct cut through the fear and carried me forward.

Grandma kept me out of school that week until Friday, when she took me during lunch break to clear out my desk, talk to my teacher about what was happening, and set me up to be homeschooled in El Dorado.

When the time came to actually leave, it broke my heart. The guilt touched every part of me. It weighed on me that I was leaving her behind, and a sense of abandonment gnawed at me, though she wasn't even there.

My uncle Rod picked me up and drove me halfway across the state to meet Troy and Pam in Hays, Kansas. They were all stepping up not only in the face of potential legal action, but at the risk of incurring their sister's bitter, long-lasting-hatred.

As we made our way east, I stared out the window of Rod's truck, pinching my skin to see if I could feel it. Double-checking that it was real. The smell of his shop was familiar, a mix of burnt metal and grease that clung to him just like it had to Grandpa.

The silence in the car was tight, crowded with everything left unsaid. I pictured what life would be like in El Dorado and what Mom's life would be without me.

Once I arrived in El Dorado, Troy and Pam set me up in the living room on the pull-out couch and I started to decompress. Living there with them, a sense of security started to take quite a weight off of my shoulders. It was clear that they would do anything they could to protect me, but the reality of the action I had taken put the weight back on me.

When things finally slowed down, it became clear that I was emotionally numb, depressed to the point I couldn't think, only exist. I wanted to laugh and joke, but I didn't have it in me.

When I was able to momentarily put aside my issues, observing their life was fascinating.

Troy was the epitome of cool for me. He stood out amongst the other members of the Butts family as an extrovert, charming anyone he made contact with, sometimes with merely a smile. His energy was sweet, but also ornery, willing to say just about anything for a laugh.

He was as smooth as I've seen anyone be, his words flowing effortlessly. Confident, without hesitation or a filter. Whether in conversation or holding court, his natural charisma commanded your attention.

Troy had light brown hair, neatly combed back, and a short, well-groomed goatee. His blue eyes were striking like Johnathan's and our Great Uncle Dan's. Even seated in his wheelchair, his height and lanky build were obvious.

Pam was short and full of energy, especially late at night. Her dark brown curly hair and expressive face were usually accompanied by a sweet smile. She loved to talk, weaving in and out of stories as she buzzed around the house. Mornings were a different story. They both had a hard time getting up, but she was notorious for hitting the snooze button until Troy hollered for her to get up, and to help him up too.

Her selflessness was obvious. Troy broke his neck not long after they got married, and from that point on, she dedicated herself to becoming his full-time caretaker.

She lifted him to and from his wheelchair and bed every morning and night, manually exercised his legs, and bathed him among so many other things.

It was by far the most successful relationship I'd ever witnessed.

Their son, Tim, was also living with them, and battling a rare genetic kidney disease called Cystinosis, a progressive and terminal illness.

He was diagnosed at one-year-old and was the first person in Kansas to be documented with the disease. Now in his early twenties, he was an ornery beam of light, just like his dad, always ready to say the one thing no one else would in front of the family.

When they would come to visit, Tim transformed our isolated lives in Goodland. He brought foul music, sketchy TV, and movies we weren't supposed to be watching—stuff he'd dug up from the far corners of the internet

Tim was short, with light brown hair, his mischievous expression beginning in his eyes and radiating throughout his entire face. I'd wait for him to wake up, or get home from work, eager to be involved in whatever he was doing.

As a family, they didn't wake up until late in the morning, hours later than I was used to. Pam would normally put Troy to bed around ten or eleven at night and she would stay up talking to her sister on the phone into the early hours of the morning.

After sleeping there for a few nights, Pam asked me if I remembered sitting up in the middle of the night, screaming for help. Her question took me by surprise. I had no memory of it.

She told me that it had been a regular occurrence since I'd arrived, describing how she would hug me and rub my back, trying to soothe me to sleep. It was deeply unsettling to realize how unaware I could be while sleeping.

At times, it was as if there were two versions of myself: one on the surface, steering the ship and oblivious to the turmoil surrounding me, and another buried deep within, fully aware, bearing the weight of it all. That inner self was trapped behind a thick pane of glass, muffled and distant, unable to communicate with the surface except through occasional, desperate screams.

During the day, Troy and Pam would take turns sitting at the table, receiving faxes from USD 352 in Goodland, and teaching me the 4th grade curriculum. The novelty wore off quickly. The lack of social interaction left me fully immersed in my schoolwork for prolonged periods. Yuck.

In the afternoon, I'd play outside in the trailer park or join Troy in his shop. Despite his limited arm mobility, he was a skilled woodworker, crafting intricate pieces such as small rocking chairs, corner shelves, and a custom wrestling ring for my wrestling figures.

Living in a stable environment was a huge relief, and spending time with Troy every day was a dream come true. His unwaveringly positive attitude was exactly what the shell-shocked boy inside me needed.

He treated me like his closest friend, guiding me with patience, encouragement, and love. No matter the size of the problem, Troy had a listening ear, making me feel valued and understood.

A few days later, back in Goodland, Mom came to pick me up from Grandma's and I was nowhere to be found. I'd learn later that Grandma told Pam about the brutal, vicious argument that followed where Mom had threatened again to put all of them in jail.

Then Mom called Troy.

I remember the phone ringing that day, her number flashing on the caller ID. My heart dropped into my stomach. When Troy answered, I could hear her furious shouting echoing from the receiver.

Troy tried to reason with her. His voice was steady at first, but she broke his composure.

He turned on his wheelchair and moved himself outside, away from the house, and for the first time, I heard the faint sounds of Troy yelling back at her.

My Uncle Mike, who was visiting, went outside and took the phone from Troy and spoke with Mom.

Soon after, Paul joined the conversation. I can't recall the exact words, they are snippets I pieced together from hushed conversations that followed, but there were grave threats exchanged between them. Despite the disturbing nature of their words, it was a relief to finally have someone defend me. Mike, as big and strong as ever, exuded an undeniable authority even over the phone.

The argument stretched on until the battery of the cordless phone they were using gave out. Without missing a beat, they switched to Mike's cell phone to continue the heated exchange.

Recently, I asked Pam about this tumultuous period. That's when I learned about the intervention I spoke of earlier, during which Pam stood her ground as my mom became confrontational and aggressive.

Pam warned her firmly, "If you come at me like that, I'll fight you."

Mom's insecurity showed as she shot back, "Pam, you think you're a better mom than me?"

Calmly, Pam responded, "At this point, I am."

Pam said from that day forward, my mom held a deep, unforgiving grudge against her.

The initial phone confrontation between the adults eventually subsided. After some time, Troy and Pam expressed it was important for me to reconnect with my mom, so they arranged for us to speak on the phone.

Hearing her voice again touched a deep, tender place in my heart. Despite everything, I realized how much I missed her.

We began to speak regularly, slowly rebuilding our relationship on a firmer foundation. Most conversations were normal, showing her in a controlled, presentable state.

Ultimately, our dialogue took a dark turn when she began hinting at taking her own life if I didn't return soon. The message was clear: without me, she was afraid of what she might do because she saw no reason to live.

That was enough for me. I packed my bags and requested to go home.

My brief escape was over, and before I knew it, I was traveling northwest to Newton, Kansas, with Troy and Pam to meet my mom and her cousin, Terri.

The drive to the meeting was fraught with a sickening tension, a sense of impending doom looming ominously in the air. The meeting itself was tense, but uneventful. Close to Troy and Pam, I could sense the intensity of my mom's ire—the type Mom described as blinding, where she couldn't see straight.

Once we were away from those who had taken me away, her demeanor shifted dramatically. She didn't blame me for anything; instead, she seemed genuinely happy to see me.

It was night, and as we drove to Goodland, I watched the highway lights blur and the road markings flicker past. Seated in the back, I occupied myself with a handheld Frogger game Mom had given to me, oblivious to the irony it represented.

CHAPTER THIRTEEN

Jason & Kalyn

Back in Goodland, the changes kept coming at Paul's house.

I learned that Paul had three kids living down in Texarkana, Texas. He actually had several others scattered around Goodland, though he never mentioned them to me.

I warn you, this is not a joke. He was so impressed with how well my mom had raised me, having turned me into a well-behaved, polite kid, that he suggested she teach him how to be a good parent. So, Jason and Kalyn, two of his boys, would be coming to live with us at 619 W 9th Street.

Jason was my age; Kalyn was a year younger.

Part of me was excited to not be alone anymore, to have someone to go through this with. I stayed with my mom to help her through this tough time in her life, but she had Paul, and I had nobody.

But another part of me was scared of how the dynamic would change. It never amounted to much, but at least with my mom and me, Paul was outnumbered. Mostly, I couldn't fully comprehend whether it would be good or bad. I thought about it constantly before they arrived, anticipating, wondering, and worrying. Knowing Paul, I assumed his kids were pretty rough, and wondered if I would become a target.

When they finally arrived, they were nothing but nice to me. Jason was confident and a little more serious, though he could be playful too when he wasn't around his dad. Kalyn was even more playful, with a younger brother energy just like me.

I was right about one thing, though, the boys were tough. They could fight, as was evident on their first day of school.

I don't remember what led up to it, but I found myself standing next to Jason and Kalyn, facing three other boys ready to brawl in a field next to the school. Before I could react, Jason had split his legs to trip the guy facing me and the other facing Kalyn, then quickly took down the one directly in front of him, and gave him a serious beating. He was reprimanded by the school, but other students took notice. Mom and Paul were glad we stood up for ourselves.

I enjoyed the time we spent together when it was just us. I knew it wasn't their fault that Paul was their dad, but having them as my friends did complicate any interaction I had with my family. With the mindset I had, I didn't feel I could mention Jason and Kalyn to people like my grandma. It was admitting guilt. Acknowledging that, yes, my mom was with Paul, and there seemed to be no end in sight.

One afternoon, Jason and Kalyn got into a squabble, and Paul's solution was as shocking as it was cruel: Jason was told to stand with his hands behind his back while Kalyn took free punches at his face. I had removed myself from the living room, but Paul noticed, and insisted that I come watch.

Seeing it play out made my skin crawl. Kalyn was in tears initially, hesitant to follow through. But after his dad's threats, he started swinging. With each punch, he seemed to discover a grim satisfaction. Jason, standing stoically, absorbed the blows until he, too, broke down into tears.

I stood there, frozen, unable to move. Guilt weighed heavily on me. Not for what happened, but for escaping punishment myself, even though I wasn't involved. The memory makes my stomach uneasy.

While writing this, I decided to search for Jason on Facebook. I hadn't found him in previous attempts, but it had been years since I last tried.

This time, I found him.

At the top of Jason's page was a video of his lifeless body on a hospital bed, a large white wrap around his head, as he was rolled down a hospital hallway. It was posted by his partner, expressing pride in him for participating in the honor walk, a ceremony where staff and loved ones honor the organ donor as they're taken to the operating room for organ retrieval.

According to his widow, Jason had taken his own life.

Stumbling upon this devastated me. I had spent so many years reflecting on the difficult experiences we shared, but I never talked to him about it. I feel guilty for having made it out, confused, wondering how I haven't met the same fate. But most of all, I have a haunting sorrow for Jason, knowing he didn't really have a chance.

CHAPTER FOURTEEN

A Cold Night In Dodge City

Around this time, an old friend of Johnathan and Josh's named Jase, and his brother Taylor, moved back to Goodland. They became a lifeline for me, something I could cling to that reminded me of the past and made me feel somewhat normal again.

Jase and Taylor became the closest thing I had to Josh and Johnathan. By then, Jase was old enough to drive and had a small, admittedly shitty, little white car. During one of our outings, the day after Halloween, we drove around Goodland listening to music, when Jase decided to do some "NASCAR driving" as he called it. He was behind the wheel, Taylor was in the passenger seat, and I was in the back passenger seat.

My seatbelt wouldn't latch properly, so I held it in place as best I could while Jase sped into the fairgrounds parking lot. He pushed the car as fast as it would go and I noticed what I believed was dirt starting to kick up in front of the windshield. That's the last thing I remember before waking up with the car on its side, the driver's door in the air.

All three of us ended up in the front passenger seat area. After we all regained consciousness, we tried to kick out the windshield so we could escape, but when that didn't work, we crawled out through a tiny opening under the passenger side door, with the car still tipped on its side.

That incident was the beginning of my distrust of riding in cars. After that, I became hesitant to ride in anyone's vehicle. Friend or foe. The last few years had already eroded my trust in people, and now I not only avoided them and using their dishes, I didn't want to get in their cars either.

Another thing I've realized is that my mom often expressed her fury through her driving. One particular instance stands out: she came to pick me up after I'd been staying with my grandma for a weekend. She decided to bring me home in a rampage, probably mid-comedown.

She stomped on the gas pedal, literally not figuratively but lifting her foot and slamming it down while crying out at the top of her lungs, and we went flying. She blew through stop signs without hesitation, and I sat frozen, terrified at what might happen next.

I went into a sort of safe mode, like an old PC infected with a virus, trying to stay as quiet and still as possible, only speaking to apologize for whatever I could imagine was wrong.

This was only the beginning. Later, after the Suburban was repossessed, we faced nonstop car troubles. Breakdowns, flat tires, and a faulty gas gauge that forced us to count how many miles we'd driven after putting five or ten dollars in, periodically miscalculating and running out of gas.

Some cars had no power steering, others had starters that gave out, leaving you demoralized as you sat there turning the key repeatedly, getting nothing. We were constantly at air pumps filling up tires that were constantly low. All things that took money to fix. Money we didn't have. Every drive turned into a stressful ordeal.

In Goodland, where a car was essential to get anywhere, this became a constant struggle.

I rarely ever said a word, but the look on my face made it clear when I felt unsafe. Mom would insist, practically spitting the words, that she'd *never* put me in danger. But after the incident in Dodge City, whatever small comfort those words once offered was completely gone.

One afternoon, Mom informed me that we, as a household, would be traveling to Dodge City, Kansas. She knew how scared I was of entering any new situation with Paul. He was truly a loose cannon, ready to explode at any moment, and any variable could cause a spiral into disaster. The thought of a three-hour drive with him and an overnight stay in an unfamiliar place filled me with terror.

The first thing she mentioned was that we'd be going go-karting. Even in safe-mode, a flicker of excitement slipped through. I was hesitant but gave in to the idea, clinging to the go-kart excitement from the moment I heard about it until the day we actually arrived at the track.

Part of me didn't believe we'd actually make it to the go-karts, expecting one of their fights to derail the plan. It was a long shot. Later, I learned that we'd also be attending Paul's grandmother's funeral, which only added to my doubt.

Much to my surprise, we made it to the track, and the go-karting was a blast. I remember starting to let my guard down and thinking, "Wow, things actually turned out pretty well this time."

After go-karting, we drove to a sheet metal building on the outskirts of Dodge City. Mom and Paul went inside while Jason, Kalyn, and I stayed in the car. Hours passed before Mom returned, almost retreating, and curled up to go to sleep in the passenger seat. I followed suit, drifting in and out of sleep, trying to stay warm as the night got colder.

I knew it was a mistake, but after so many hours in that Suburban—body aching, hands twitching, thoughts looping with no way out—I was starting to come apart from the inside.

The silence had a hum to it, and every breath, every beat of my heart, snagged. Like it was catching on something sharp. I couldn't sit there any longer. If I didn't move, didn't act, I was afraid I might lose it for good.

Stupidly, I decided to make a move. I crept up the gravel driveway and slipped into the building. Inside, the dim light barely exposed the clutter and disarray.

The entire place was stained with neglect and the stale stench of alcohol and cigarettes.

My heart raced as I moved deeper inside, the darkness pressing in around me. There, in the back room, Paul and his ghouls were playing cards, their movements slow and disconnected, as if they were lost in their own individual worlds. Some of them looked half-dead, with hollow cheeks, twitchy eyes, and skin that seemed too thin.

The air was thick with tension.

I stepped in quietly. They barely registered my presence. Or perhaps deliberately avoided it.

No one said a word. A deep sense of unease crept over me, so I turned around and started to slowly make my way back to the car.

I left the room and walked toward the car, my pace steady at first, but as the unease grew, my steps quickened until I found myself breaking into a run, the urgency to escape swallowing me.

Everyone in the car was asleep when I returned, so I resigned myself to try my best to do the same.

I had barely drifted off when I was jolted awake by the sound of the driver's door slamming. Paul threw himself in the driver's seat of the Suburban. He was heavy with silence—the kind that only came before an explosion.

He turned the ignition, and for a second, he didn't move. He stared through the windshield, his breathing heavy, his fingers flexing on the wheel. Whatever was about to happen had already started.

Suddenly, without warning, he threw the Suburban into reverse and slammed his foot on the gas.

We went flying through the parking lot, gravel hammering against the undercarriage, the whole car shuddering like it might come apart. No one spoke words; we all screamed. Including Paul.

This was the angriest I'd ever seen him and he held my life in his hands more directly than ever before. There were so many dangerous situations that I convinced myself I had avoided by becoming a person that wouldn't upset even the most paranoid meth addict. Reading their moods, adjusting my energy to match theirs, agreeing with whatever kept them happy. Perfect tone, perfect words, perfect silence when called for.

Not tonight.

The tires hadn't even stopped screeching when Paul jammed it into drive, hurling us forward even faster. Rocks exploded in all directions as we screamed, the tires shrieking, fighting for grip but slipping helplessly against the loose gravel beneath them.

Paul started yanking the steering wheel side to side with a wild intensity, the car lurching violently with each sharp turn. My body slammed against the door and the cold window in one direction and back again, the seat belt cutting into my ribs, his foot continued to press the pedal to the floor.

My ears began to ring as I tried to focus on the situation I was in. My brain couldn't keep up. Was this real? Was this actually happening?

I didn't know what else to do, so grasping for anything, I cried out, raw and desperate.

"I'm sorry! I'm sorry!"

I wasn't sure what I was apologizing for, but it was the only thing I could think of that might diffuse the situation.

That's when he snapped his head back, looking directly at me, and yelled, "YOU!"

When I saw his face, it wasn't human. I was looking at a monster. His eyes were boiling. Pits of rage that were endless. It wasn't simply anger, it was cursed, ancient, as if I'd wronged him for a thousand lifetimes and he had finally caught up to me. He didn't want to kill me, he wanted me to suffer first. Whatever had taken hold of him dissolved whatever was left of the person, leaving only hatred for me behind.

I don't remember exactly what he said, but it came out in violent bursts, a garbled mess of 'you motherfucker this, you piece of shit that,' words slurred but cutting.

And I truly had no idea why this was happening or why my apology made things worse. Maybe he saw it as me mocking him, or that I had some kind of sick satisfaction in saying it. Maybe I had walked into that shack at the wrong time and caught a glimpse of what was meant to stay hidden.

Or maybe there was no reason at all.

But Paul wasn't done.

"I'm gonna kill every single one of us tonight!"

The words came out with power, conviction, as if saying them out loud made them real, made him stronger.

Paul straightened the wheel, locked onto the exit of the parking lot, and again slammed the gas. The tires squealed, rubber burning as we shot onto the road.

"We are gonna fucking die tonight!" he shouted.

Paul whipped the Suburban across the empty highway, veering recklessly over the lanes, playing with our lives. The wails of me, Mom, Jason, and Kalyn blended into the chaos and dissolved into white noise.

The whole car started to lift, just enough for my stomach to drop, before slamming back down, rocking on its suspension as we fishtailed wildly across the highway. Every sharp turn shoved us against the doors, the ditch looming closer each time. The world around me was barely holding on.

"I'm gonna roll this fucking bitch!" Paul yelled, his voice frantic and unhinged.

At that moment, I knew. This was it. I was about to die.

The realization wasn't a desperate yelp in my head, it was quiet. I couldn't fight it. No matter how hard I tried to figure out how to make this stop. I couldn't stop it. I had to accept it.

I looked at my mom, curled up in the front seat, trembling in fear but not telling him to stop, helplessly accepting what was happening.

Jason and Kalyn were sitting together; Jason was a protective older brother, holding Kalyn as close as he could as they both screamed and wept.

I sat alone, turning inward, trying to figure out how to comfort myself in what I was sure were my last moments.

For a second, my mind drifted, grasping for anything familiar, anything that felt safe.

I thought about all the times I had sat in this same seat before. Paul wasn't driving. My dad was. Johnathan and Josh were next to me. Mom was up front in the passenger seat, but she wasn't crying. She was laughing.

I remembered we drove the Suburban all the way to Cordova, Alabama together. Our longest road trip. The image of stopping at a gas station overnight washed over me. It was the first I can remember seeing 2:00 a.m. I couldn't help thinking that it was so *cool.*

I thought about all the afternoons before everything fell apart when Mom picked me up from school, and I sat in this same seat, hearing the same question: 'What did you learn at school today?'

I remembered that this was the seat where I fell in love with music, where I heard Eddie Vedder sing my name in a song on the way to Bonny Lake, where I learned the distinctive sound when Neil Peart beat on his drums.

But that's all they were now. Memories.

I wasn't religious, but in that moment, all I could do was pray to anyone who might be listening. Begging. Help me survive this. Or at least make it to the next life safely.

The Suburban tore down the highway, jerking violently as Paul swerved, except something had changed. The road ahead of us no longer looked the same. Headlights appeared in the distance. The dark emptiness of the highway gave way to scattered streetlights and the faint glow of the city limits.

Paul went silent.

The screaming, the threats, all of it just stopped. But the way he gripped the wheel, the way his foot stayed heavy on the gas, told me it wasn't over. The erratic movements didn't stop, they shifted. Less wild, more controlled, but still angry and unpredictable.

I had no idea where he was taking us.

And I never would have guessed it was McDonald's.

Out of nowhere, Paul whipped the Suburban into the parking lot at an unthinkable speed and stopped hard. The golden arches stared down at us in the drive-through line as if nothing had happened, like we hadn't spent the last few minutes flirting with death.

I was beyond confused. The terror had not left me. Or anyone else in the car. We all stayed completely silent.

I don't remember hearing him say anything as he ordered, but he must have. Paul floored the gas from the speaker to the window, tires squealing and making a scene. Paul grabbed our food without a word from anyone else in the car. We sat there frozen.

He drove us across town as fast as he could, snapping back into his psychosis. After blowing through countless stop signs, we pulled into a broken-down motel. He put the Suburban in park and went inside.

We were all silent—including Mom.

Paul returned with a white piece of paper and a room key, parking the car as if it were any other night. Like we hadn't spent the last hour trying not to die. Like nothing had happened.

No acknowledgement of the terror he'd put us through.

Paul grabbed the McDonald's bag and disappeared into the room. He sat and ate. We weren't even there to him. Not that any of us would've had the appetite anyway.

I don't remember anything else from that night. Not a single thought, not a moment where I let my guard down.

I didn't walk away from Dodge City the same. No, I didn't become religious. Reaching out only when I needed help seemed wrong. Paul didn't kill us, but he showed me how close to the surface that was for him, and how he could be pushed to the edge of executing it with one wrong comment. How easy it would have been for him.

I also struggled with the fact that my mom didn't do anything to stop him. Maybe she stayed quiet to keep things from escalating, but in that moment, I was completely alone in what I was sure were my last moments.

None of us ever spoke about it afterward. I couldn't bring myself to be honest with my mom. She was at the heart of so many of my struggles, yet the thought of telling her was unbearable. I really didn't want to hurt her.

I couldn't confide in my grandma or cousin Summer either. Mom had made it clear, both in words and actions, that our business was to stay with us. To share what happened was putting her down, betraying her, airing out our dirty laundry.

I might sound bitter now, but back then, I wasn't. I was loyal. Quietly, endlessly, desperately loyal. I gave her all the love I had, hoping it would be enough to fix things. Hoping it would be enough to make a difference. But a lot of times, that love was met with outright rejection. When I tried to comfort her in her tears, she would push me away, her eyes flashing with a fierce hostility that left me stunned. I'd run off, in tears myself, confused and hurt.

My life had become a maze of confusion.

Chapter Fifteen

Grandma & Nathan

After the incident in Dodge City, Paul's daughter Jessica, also from Texarkana, came to live with us. Like her brothers, we got along easily. However, our time living together was brief, because not long after I ended up going to stay with my grandma.

I don't remember if I requested to go or if Mom suggested it, but it wasn't supposed to be for long. Only a few days. But I stayed much longer, probably almost a year.

My grandma's house at 206 Broadway was a sanctuary, a place where the chaos of the world couldn't reach me. Her love was a warm embrace, wrapping around me with a fierce, protective strength.

When she looked at me, her eyes held a depth of understanding that made me feel truly seen, unconditionally loved, and completely safe. Grandma was slender, with a prominent nose and a darker complexion than the rest of us. She had strong, defined bone structure that felt carved, something timeless in her face, with a quiet strength behind her eyes. She wore false teeth and flashed a wide, confident smile. Her hair was short and usually styled in a perm.

She only raised her voice during lighthearted teasing with my cousin Nathan, who was living with her.

Nathan had been severely injured in a car accident as a child, which tragically killed his mother and badly hurt his sister, Summer. The accident left him with a significant brain injury. After that, all he could really say were a few words: 'Hi,'

'Bye,' 'Yep,' and 'Nope.' His learning abilities were severely impaired, and he required a caretaker, in this case, Grandma.

The bond between them was unique and strong. She brought more depth to his life, taking the time to understand him and finding ways to make a positive difference. Some things were big, acting as his caretaker, other things were small, like calling him 'George,' which never failed to get a smile in response.

To this day, I love Nathan with everything I have. We bonded over simple joys, watching *SpongeBob* together, laughing at the same silly moments. His favorite movie was *Joe Dirt*, and Grandma had a worn VHS copy that he insisted we play every single day during the summer without fail. From the opening credits, when the licks of *Sweet Home Alabama* poured out from the TV, Nathan would light up, his whole body jolting with excitement. He'd clap his hands and glance over at me, his eyes wide, looking to see if I knew what he was so thrilled about.

Before too long, I learned exactly what he was trying to tell me. He could sense when someone nodded along instead of listening to him, and it upset him deeply. It was hard to witness because I knew, deep down, he had the same longing to connect and be heard as anyone else, but his words were trapped inside.

Nathan stood about 5'8" and weighed over 200 pounds, with short brown curls that were beginning to thin at the crown. His thick glasses framed his full, rounded face, giving him a gentle, contemplative look, but it was his smile that defined him, spreading across his entire face and radiating a warmth and joy that could light up the room.

When I picture him, he's wearing a tank top, jean shorts, and sandals, his feet marked by the strongest sandal tans you've ever seen.

Nathan also had a seizure disorder. When the seizures came, his body would tremble and convulse violently. I'd watch as Grandma would rush to sit on his lap, wrap him in a tight embrace, and softly reassure him that everything was alright, that she was there. Slowly, indiscernibly at first, he would begin to calm down, gradually returning to himself.

But the aftermath was hard. If you asked if he was feeling okay, he'd nod yes, but the pain and exhaustion were written on his face. Seeing that broke my heart.

I took on that role whenever I could, sitting on his lap, hugging him close, and helping to bring him back to reality. It was terrifying to feel his body convulse, but it was the least I could do for him in his time of need.

The seizures improved for a period, but returned in an unexpected form. He no longer visibly shook, but his eyes would gloss over, his body would freeze, and he'd tense up. These episodes became more frequent, and when he came to, his anger was explosive.

Sometimes it started with him standing up, talking to himself, saying 'No.' The tone and inflection varied, like he was having a conversation with someone in his head, someone he was upset with. It began calmly but would escalate into violence. He'd throw drinking glasses across the room, roaring, 'NO!'

When I was in the room, I could usually sense the signs and get out of the house before he became angry. But if I was in another room and didn't catch it quickly enough, I'd end up trapped, sometimes hiding in the back of my closet. Other times, I had to sprint past him to escape out the front or rear door as he chased me, slamming and locking the door behind me.

I don't blame him. I know he was dealing with things on the inside that we couldn't imagine, but for a period of time, his frustration was often directed at me, as if he didn't want me there. He wanted it to be just him and Grandma. That's it. Not all the time, most often we were best friends, brothers, but when his seizures hit, all his worst feelings about me seemed to come out. He grabbed and pushed me a few times, but I was able to escape pretty easily.

His exasperation wasn't only directed at me; it was also aimed at Grandma. Maybe more, because she didn't run away. He threw things at her, pushed, and grabbed her too.

In a moment of sudden chaos, Nathan flew into one of his episodes, and I couldn't escape the house in time. He chased me down, backing me into a corner before turning his focus to Grandma, who was desperately trying to distract him, like a rodeo clown dodging a bull.

He cornered her as she tried to open the doors to get out of the house herself, and I could see imminent violence about to unfold.

I stood frozen, gripped by overpowering stress.

Grandma was 5'7" and weighed maybe 97 pounds, dealing with her own medical issues after falling and breaking her hip, which devastated her overall health. And Nathan was about to crush her.

I had no choice but to step in between them to try and save her. Not because I was an intimidating child, but because I was the only one there. I stood in between them not sure what would happen next, but Grandma managed to get outside and Nathan pushed me aside and followed her.

Grandma eventually calmed him down, and the day returned to normal, but for the rest of my time there, I had to keep one eye open. The house was small, with few places to hide, but thankfully, I had already mastered the art of becoming invisible.

Despite all of that, I truly loved living with Grandma. She was there to pick me up after school, never missing a single day, always 15 or 20 minutes early so I didn't have to wait.

Once a week, she'd take Nathan and me out for hamburgers. On the other nights, she prepared food around 4:45 or 5 PM, nice and early, and we'd sit down together for dinner. Afterward, she'd clean up by herself, despite my offers to help, and get ready for bed. Sometimes, I followed her routine; other times, I'd be outside playing with the neighbor kids.

Overall, I was just a kid. I watched a ton of cable TV, a luxury I hadn't had since we left 240 Walnut. I got to watch *Pinky and the Brain* after school, *Monday Night Raw* every Monday night, and started a lifelong obsession with the current events as I watched the devastation of Hurricane Katrina live on CNN.

I had a routine. I was happy, and I was safe.

Even when tornado warnings were issued and I happened to be somewhere with a basement, I'd insist on returning to Grandma's, where there was no basement, willing to face the storm to be with her. I considered myself much safer huddled in her tiny bathroom, a mattress pulled over us in the bathtub, as the tornado sirens blared outside.

The 972-square-foot, two-bedroom, one-bathroom house at 206 Broadway was my dream home, even though it was in a deep state of disrepair. The ceiling was collapsing in the back room, and the bathroom was barely functional, with a pair of pliers serving as the handle for the shower faucet.

My grandma didn't really have the money to buy me new clothes on top of taking care of all my other needs, but when my cousin Summer came home, she would notice that I had 'high water jeans' or t-shirts that were either ripped or too small and would take me to buy new clothes. She said it bothered her that other kids might make fun of me. That never bothered me, but reeking like cigarettes did, and with every adult around me smoking, I didn't stand a chance.

This period with her and Nathan was invaluable. It allowed me to reclaim my childhood, to immerse myself in the simple joys of being a kid, if only for a little while.

Most days, I would come home from school and play football with myself in the front yard. I was the quarterback, receiver, referee, and announcer. I played as multiple teams, acting as different players on each one. It sounds sad, but I was having a blast.

I didn't have many close friends, but the neighborhood kids around my age and I became close. I spent time with Jaron, a neighbor, playing his favorite military-style role playing games in the backyard, using whatever we could find to add to the story.

Later, another friend, Alexandria, and her sister Ashleigh, moved in across the street, and we became fast friends. We'd explore the small neighborhood, and sometimes beyond, always finding ourselves on some new adventure.

I'm not sure who, but someone gave me an MP3 player as a gift, and I was able to download some songs from the internet. It was great, but the MP3 player was stuck on one song no matter what button I pressed, "Face Up" by Rush.

I love Rush. They are by far my favorite band, and I would have probably loved that song, but it became unbearable. Even so, listening to Rush was the closest I could get to advice from my dad, as if he were talking to me through the song, and passing along his wisdom.

For example, these lyrics: "I know it makes no difference to what you're going through, but I see the tip of the iceberg, and I worry about you," and "These changes aren't permanent, but change is."

I rode my bike all over Goodland, to and from school, to the park, to the library to use the computer, and sometimes to enjoy a nice day. To me, it might as well have been the Wild West. The streets were quiet and open, yet not entirely safe.

Loose dogs were a constant problem for me growing up. They loved to chase me. Looking back, I realize I was at least half the problem, but that didn't change what had happened.

One afternoon, I was riding to Grandma's from school when a wild dog shot out of a yard at full speed, barking, teeth bared, coming straight for me. I pedaled as fast as I could, but he was gaining, snapping at my back tire as he caught up with me. Luckily, a good Samaritan, out watering his lawn, turned his hose into the street. For reasons I still don't understand, the dog stopped in its tracks, not crossing where the water had splashed down. I didn't question it. I kept riding, yelling 'Thank you!' over my shoulder.

Another time, a dog eerily reminiscent of Beast from *The Sandlot* came after me. This one wasn't sprinting, purely stalking, but it made me stop in my tracks. He walked up to me, growling, and started nosing around the perimeter of me and my bike.

I was rooted to the spot, every muscle locked, my heart hot, as the dog circled and sniffed me, tense and bracing for the bite that might come next.

Mercifully, he lost interest and walked away.

Even when I was *almost* to Grandma's, I wasn't safe. One afternoon, as I rode up to 2nd Street, I spotted a dog standing in my grandma's driveway. Thinking that I could outsmart him, I hit a U-turn, cut through the alley, and tried to sneak in the back way. But when I got there he was already waiting for me.

Trying to outsmart him, I headed for the front again, then changed course halfway and doubled back toward the alley. At the last second, I ditched my bike and sprinted for my life, barely making it through Grandma's door before the dog closed in.

When I finally started to get a handle on the ground, the attacks started coming from the sky.

One summer, a family of Mississippi Kites decided to nest in the big tree out in front of 206 Broadway. We realized this when they began dive-bombing us every time we left or returned to the house. This wasn't playful swooping. They locked in, turned their wings inward, and torpedoed at us at full speed, sometimes making hard contact with the back of our heads.

They were pissed that we were anywhere near their nest while their babies were hatching. We couldn't even check the mail in peace.

Despite the wildlife, Grandma created an all-loving environment inside, the closest thing I had to true shelter. She was on my side every single time, even when she probably shouldn't have been.

When I was getting ready for my learner's permit, she let me back her car out of the garage. Somehow, I screwed it up and scraped the car against the garage wall. I panicked. She was the last person I wanted to upset. But when I told her, she couldn't have cared less. She was on my side, blaming the car and the garage if anything. I'm only now understanding that she showed me that she was concerned for me and not her paint job.

The first time I had a girlfriend over, her mom came inside and pleaded with Grandma to keep an eye on us at all times. Grandma assured her that she would. As soon as the mom was out of sight, Grandma closed the door to her room and didn't come out while my girlfriend was there. For a teenage boy, it was a dream come true.

Unfortunately, the good times didn't last long; Mom decided I needed to come home. She didn't ask. She resorted to the same relentless tactics to lure me back. I was constantly under pressure, burdened with the responsibility of giving her a reason to continue on. She often reminded me that without me, she would have no purpose, no reason to live. I heard this repeatedly, especially when I found her crying alone in her room.

Of all the manipulation I faced growing up, this left the most enduring scars, shaping my daily life in ways I may never fully escape. Its impact didn't stop with her. It seeped into every interaction, shaped how I saw the world, and colored my view of every loved one since.

My mom wasn't just nasty to me; whenever anyone else got involved with helping me, she would begin to hate them, believing they were going to take me away.

When Grandma was on her bad side, Mom was so nasty to her that Grandma changed her phone number and made it unlisted in the phone book to escape her wrath. She kept what was said during those calls to herself, trying her best to protect me, but I was usually the one passing the phone to her after I was torn down to tears, so Mom could continue her tirade.

I had a body and mind exploding with emotions, but I couldn't express them. Not only would they not be received by the person I needed them most, but they would also be met with anger, accusations, and guilt-tripping.

I wanted to confide in Grandma, or Summer, or anyone really, but that part of me was dead. The words were stuck somewhere deeper than my throat. If I could've pulled them out, I wouldn't have said them. I wanted to protect my mom, because no matter what she had done, I had watched her, the most important person in my life, fall to pieces.

Despite my initial reluctance, her efforts to bring me home succeeded. Before I knew it, I was once again caught in the turmoil with her and Paul, feeling miserable. Her paranoia only deepened, fueled by the doubt and hesitation she sensed in my return.

Chapter Sixteen

Handy Towers

Before I was called back to 619 W 9th Street, a mysterious rash appeared on my torso, leading to a diagnosis of shingles, an uncommon condition for children. The doctor inquired if I was under a lot of stress, and Grandma, with shame in her eyes, nodded yes in response.

Not long after this, Summer moved home to Goodland while her husband was away for military training. Even as she grew older, went away for college, and to get married, Summer made time for me when she came to visit. She would take me out for food, buy me those new pairs of jeans, or arrange for donations from her in-laws.

When she moved home, what started as a few nights staying with her gradually extended into a week, then a few weeks. It was a dream come true. At first, Mom didn't seem to mind, but as time passed, tension began to creep in, hinting at the storm brewing beneath the surface. That unease was emanating from Mom, who had grown suspicious of Summer and was ready to snap.

Years later, Summer told me that the first time she was ever called a cunt was by my mom.

I remember that day. I was sitting next to Summer while Mom was on the phone, instructing me on what to say. I couldn't bring myself to repeat her words, so Mom demanded that I hand the phone to Summer, and all hell broke loose. She unleashed an unforgivable tirade on Summer, all because she was helping me.

When I talk with Summer in the present day, she remembers the deep helplessness. Legally, her hands were tied. My mom's threats seemed to carry the weight of the law. All she could do was watch as I cried, powerless to make things better.

After returning from Summer's, the nightmare at 619 W 9th Street continued. The only difference I noticed was Paul's 1999 two-door silver Chevy Tahoe sitting in the driveway. Who knows if he already had it stowed away before he met Mom, or if he bought it using my child support money.

One of the endless arguments between her and Paul escalated to the point where my mom burst into my room, her face twisted with pain, and told me to grab my things because we were getting kicked out.

This is exactly what I dreaded when we left 240 Walnut. I knew that if things got bad enough, Mom and I would be the ones thrown out because Paul wasn't staying with us anymore; we were staying with him.

My mom was hysterical, not just angry at Paul for whatever had sparked this latest fight, but also consumed by the adrenaline from the chaos we were thrust into. Paul continued to make it clear: we had to get the fuck out.

In a frantic rush, we grabbed whatever we could and fled, the door slamming behind us. Paul had given us until morning to get the rest of our stuff, and after that, he'd start dumping it on the lawn.

We had only one place to turn: Grandma.

Mom was enraged and humiliated, knowing she had to face the true reality that she'd worked so hard to disguise and ask for forgiveness.

We drove to my grandma's late that night. My mom went straight to Grandma's room, shutting the door behind her to talk. I didn't mind. In a twisted way, one of my wishes had come true. We had left 619 W 9th Street.

The next morning, Paul dumped all our belongings, everything he hadn't stolen, on the front lawn. We didn't have much there, most of our bigger items were still in storage, but picking up your things from the ground and cramming them into our vehicle was humiliating. Years later, I would realize how much we'd lost when I came across some of my childhood toys while visiting a friend of Paul's.

My sense of security, already fragile, was obliterated, leaving me more exposed and vulnerable than ever before. It's been a never-ending feeling that I still struggle to shake to this day. It continues to linger deep into my adult life, turning every move from one apartment or house to another into a nerve-wracking ordeal, prodding wounds that never had a chance to heal. Even when I have security, I can't convince myself of it.

We stayed at my grandma's for a few weeks. Paul and Mom had fought viciously almost constantly, and sometimes he would disappear for days or even a week, but this time didn't cycle the way the others had. Mom was finally admitting she needed to make a change, to leave him. It was the one thing I had begged for, in the rare moments I could find the words.

I was happy to stay with Grandma, but it was clear that staying there weighed heavily on my mom. Beyond everything else, not having her own space was a failure to her.

My mom had been in a dark place for quite a while, making bad decisions that put us in dangerous situations. But even in those times, she had moments of resilience. She got us on the waitlist for a low-income housing agency in Goodland, and the idea of having our own place, free from Paul, felt too good to be true.

A few weeks later, we got the news. We were approved to be the first tenants in Handy Towers, a building that had previously been a senior-only living facility. Being the poor kid at school was nothing new, but this was taking it to a new level. We knew we would stick out and expected to be judged and watched closely.

But I didn't care. This place was heaven to me. Not only was it ours, not Paul's, but the security was everything I hoped for in my neurotic state. A key card was needed to get through the double doors downstairs, and we were on the third floor, behind a thick wooden door, far removed from any threat that might come our way. The building was a large, solid brick structure, rugged enough that even if Paul wanted to burn it down, it wouldn't be easy.

Despite everything she had put me through in those last few years, I couldn't have been more proud of my mom for this. It was long overdue, but we had finally found a place of safety. We pulled our old couch and beds out of storage and did our best to furnish our little apartment.

With just me and my mom, life worked so well. We got along almost perfectly, and she started doing motherly things again, like sitting and coloring with me. I started to relax, feeling triumphant that we had escaped Paul's grip.

Despite that sense of relief, we were still incredibly poor and this might have been our lowest point. Mom was asking me to bring home rolls of toilet paper from Grandma's because we couldn't afford any. She would send me to Grandma's for dinner as often as she could, relying heavily on free school breakfast and lunches. For reasons I can't fully grasp, we didn't get food stamps until years later. During those moments of scarcity, Mom and I would engage in a silent dance of self-sacrifice, each of us pretending to be full, hoping the other would eat.

Things went well for a while. Maybe a month or two. I'm not sure exactly when or how it happened, but one day, Paul was simply back.

Mom would give me sheepish looks, fully aware that I was devastated by his return, knowing how much better we were without him. But I had no control over it. Whenever I spoke up, she would either cry about dying alone or remind me that she was the adult.

By now, Jason and Jessica had gone back to Texas. Kalyn stayed in Goodland, though he didn't live with us at Handy Towers. I'm guessing he stayed with his grandparents, but he was still around a lot. As we left the apartment one day, I remember him growing frustrated with my ignorance about my mom and his dad's drug use.

"You know what they're doing in there, right?" he said, his voice edged with frustration and disgust.

I stayed silent. My mom didn't want me to know, and I didn't want to know. As long as I didn't see it with my own eyes, I could maintain a fragile sense of denial, a way to shield myself from the truth.

Paul's return shattered my hope. This was the regular cycle—escaping Paul's grip, only to be dragged in again. It was a horrible feeling, but all too familiar, knowing that even when things are good in my life, the darkness isn't far behind.

Chapter Seventeen

Escape To Rapid City

In 2007, my freshman year of high school, a new guy, Kelly, enrolled into USD 352 in Goodland. He was loud and cocky. In class, he'd shake his leg so vigorously that it rattled the whole classroom floor. I hadn't really interacted with him, but from spending time around him for a short time, I knew I didn't like him.

His face was marked by a confident smirk and undeniable orneriness. His short, light brown hair was casually messy, and a hint of stubble gave him an edge, adding to his confidence and his bold presence.

While I was living at my grandma's, I had started to develop a real love for football, particularly the Dallas Cowboys. My grandma was a huge fan, and she would lovingly talk about memories of watching her favorite, Roger Staubach. To her, they were heroes. That year, my uncle Troy gave me a Dallas Cowboys shirt for my birthday.

One day, I wore that shirt to class, and Kelly approached me, asking if I liked the Cowboys. I told him I did, and from that moment on, we became friends.

Another guy in our class, Chris, was also a Cowboys fan. He and Kelly were already friends. I had known Chris for years; we'd hung out before, but weren't close.

Chris had an easy, athletic confidence about him, the kind of presence that made him seem both laid-back and ready for a fight. His dark eyes held a quiet intensity, both sharp and observant, but his broad, unguarded smile softened him.

One night, the three of us planned to meet up at the bowling alley to watch the Cowboys and Seahawks play in the playoffs. That night, our bond was sealed as we left the bowling alley in tears, mocked by the other patrons, devastated after Tony Romo dropped the snap for the kick and the Cowboys lost.

From that moment on, we were inseparable. It was us against the world.

Having Kelly and Chris as friends made all the difference in my life. The tension in my body eased knowing I wasn't in it alone. They lifted me up, bringing me to life once again—not just to survive, but to feel alive, if only for a limited time.

We spent so much of our day-to-day lives together, had each other's backs in school arguments, and talked endlessly about the Cowboys—the kind of details most people ignored, like which backup linemen had the best footwork in pass protection or which receivers rounded off their slant routes and blew timing.

Kelly was the new kid, but it really didn't seem like it. He was bold, loud-mouthed, and not the one to back down from any confrontation.

Chris was smooth, almost too smooth—the kind of guy who could win anyone over with a smile. He was laid-back and naturally charismatic. But when it came down to it, he could be a savage. I'd seen it. He could flip in a second if he had to defend himself. Neither of them came from prestigious Goodland families, but they refused to be seen as less than when pushed by our classmates.

We spent hours playing catch with a football in the front yard or at Gulick or Chambers Park. We walked everywhere and found every free activity we could. And when it wasn't free, we scraped and schemed to pull together the cash for things like a ticket to the high school football game or a movie at the Sherman Theatre. Whatever it was, we made the most of it, riding the high of youth.

Even so, the problems before persisted: desperate poverty and a volatile home life with Mom and Paul. But my support system was growing, even if we didn't openly talk about what was happening.

The next few months would test that.

There were multiple instances when Mom wouldn't come home for days. Thankfully, now I was old enough to have keys.

I would call again and again, the ringing stretching into nothing, looping endlessly, each unanswered ring echoing into a vast, empty dark.

The sound of that ringing gives me anxiety whenever I make a call in the present day.

I cycled through every emotion. Terror that she might be dead, loneliness, and the bitterness of being left like this. I had enough time to feel them all.

At the bottom of that well of despair, I had finally had enough of this life. Enough of the chaos, the fear, the pretending.

Even in calm moments, I was bracing for impact.

Sleep was no longer restful.

And for what? She wasn't here.

Then my mind went to my dad. Where was he right now? Did he ever wonder the same about me? How about my brothers? I remembered the last letter he wrote me and how much it had meant. Proof he still cared. Proof that I wasn't forgotten.

After years of distance, I was tired of the feeling of not knowing my own father.

By now, my brothers were finishing up high school in Washington, and Dad had moved to Rapid City, South Dakota for work.

After she returned again without explanation, I waited for the right moment of my courage and her mood to line up, and told Mom that I felt like I didn't know my dad and I wanted to go live with him.

Which was true. But if I were able to tell her the truth that day, I would have said more than that. I would have told her that my drive to stay was withering when she had abandoned me so many times, while Dad was out there, ready and willing to take care of me.

He and I kept in touch mostly through those letters and occasional phone calls when I was with Grandma, Troy, or Summer. I missed him desperately. When the coast was clear, he made it a point to tell me that I could come live with him.

At first, it almost seemed like a good excuse for me to have to leave. But the feeling began to gnaw at me. He had been away so much when I was a kid, traveling for work, and he left when I was nine to take care of my brothers. I held no resentment. I knew he did the right thing in getting them as far away from her and Paul as possible and giving them a stable environment to grow up in. But now, at fourteen, his absence left an emptiness inside of me that I could no longer ignore.

When I told my mom I wanted to leave, she was devastated. Not just in the moment, but for days and weeks afterward. One moment, she was cold and distant, the next, she was raging, furious at me for suggesting it. Other times, she was angry, but with tears in her eyes.

She made it clear how heartbroken she was and that she would stay that way until I returned. Her persistence wore me down, and we agreed that I would give it a try for the rest of the school year, returning to Goodland before making any final decisions.

In a last-ditch effort to get me to stay, she asked if I was sure and reminded me of everything I had in Goodland—my grandma, my two new friends, and all I had ever known—but I stood firm and asked Dad to come get me.

After making sure I was serious, he wasted no time making plans to drive to Goodland.

This was the first time in years that Paul or Mom had been anywhere near Dad. The idea alone had my stomach in knots.

When the day finally came, it was hard to tell what she was saying through all the crying. Her face blotchy, her movements frantic, she looked lost in her own house. I was doing my damndest to hold strong, but it was gut-wrenching packing my things, peeling away pieces of a life we'd built together. It wasn't rushed, wasn't dramatic, just a long silent goodbye. Each zip of a bag was another nail, sealing her coffin shut. I couldn't believe I was finally doing it.

When Dad pulled up in his rental car, through some miracle, Paul was nowhere to be found. Adrenaline was pumping for Mom, but their meeting was cordial. Dad was guarded, but on this day, Mom wasn't thinking about their divorce, or Paul, she was thinking about me.

They didn't speak much, but I do remember one interaction.

"Take good care of him." Mom muttered through a breaking voice.

"I will." Dad replied, in a voice that conveyed peace.

My goodbye hug with Mom came with a weight so crushing that I wasn't sure my legs would keep me upright.

I fought every instinct to stay wrapped in her arms, the first place that I ever belonged.

But my gut told me it was time to leave.

She stood outside as we drove away, her face contorted, soaked with tears, and waved. Growing smaller in the distance but never truly fading.

I was grateful for my sunglasses that day. They hid the tears falling down my face, the ones that would have shattered the tough front I had on for Dad.

Dad was set on getting out of Goodland fast, unwilling to linger long enough for anyone to drag him into the chaos. So we kept moving. No pauses. No second glances.

The further we got from Goodland, the quieter my mind became. Less scanning for warning signs, less bracing. I was listening to the hum of the engine and the sound of Rush through the speakers.

The land stretched endlessly, the sky the same, broken only by clusters of white grain elevators, exactly as Truman Capote once described.

As I relaxed in the calming presence of my dad, a trait I hoped I've inherited, he slowed the car and took an exit. We were somewhere in Northeast Colorado.

We pulled into the truck stop, a sprawl of pavement and long rows of pumps, semis parked in neat lines. A few travelers milled about, some stretching their legs, others lingering off to the side with a cigarette, all moving with the slow, deliberate pace of people fighting through a long drive.

Dad eased up to the pump, braking smoothly as the car settled into place.

As the car settled and I adjusted to the stillness, I noticed a familiar vehicle parked in front of the store: a 1999 two-door, silver Chevy Tahoe.

My heart and stomach sank. No fucking way, I thought.

But I saw him walking toward the store. Baseball cap, semi-rimless baseball-style sunglasses, the kind you'd see on a baseball coach or hanging on a gas station rack, and a rough cut-off t-shirt.

It was Paul.

Unaware of the situation, my dad pumped gas, then pulled into a parking spot at the front of the building and headed around back for a cigarette, telling me to go inside for a snack and a bathroom break.

My heart raced and my mind spun as I tried to figure out what to do, expecting Paul and his goons to follow him.

I froze. Should I tell him? If I did, would it make it worse?

That hate had been brewing for years. I'm not sure what Paul had to be angry about, but my dad had a deep well to pull from for the man who had callously destroyed his and his children's lives.

As much history as there was between them, I wasn't sure Dad actually knew what Paul looked like. But Paul had seen my dad when he invaded our home, and my dad's face still hung there on the wall in our family photos.

Aside from that, Dad stood out, especially in the Midwest.

I didn't want to get out of the car, but I didn't want to leave Dad alone either. I wasn't big enough to help, but I couldn't just sit there.

When I finally opened the door, there was Paul, standing in the aisle. My chest tightened and for a moment, I couldn't move.

Dad walked in from the back and headed straight to the restroom, still oblivious.

My mind scrambled at what to do. I didn't want Paul to see me. I tried to avoid him, but there was no chance.

He walked right towards me.

I was rooted to the spot, every muscle locked, my heart hot, bracing for what might come next.

Paul kept walking, ignoring me as if he didn't recognize me. As he passed by me in the aisleway, heat radiated off of him, an electric charge in the air, poisoned and rotten, leaving me cold in his wake.

I was shocked, my muscles still locked in the same spot.

Paul exited the gas station without buying anything and returned to his truck, where his goons were loitering.

Each passing second was a lifetime as I watched Dad casually pick out his drink and snack for the next leg of the drive. I had to stay calm, but all I wanted was to snap at him to hurry up, to get us the fuck out of there. My hands were shaking as I grabbed my drink and snack, meeting Dad at the counter, trying to steady myself long enough to place them down.

We headed toward the front exit, where Paul was parked. I braced for the confrontation I thought was inevitable. But as we walked to the car, nothing interrupted us. We got in, buckled our seatbelts, and backed out of the spot, my legs tingling from the rush of escape and the adrenaline pumping through me.

As we crept through the parking lot, the silence was interrupted.

"Fucking pussy!" Paul shouted from his truck.

My dad, somewhat used to experiencing ridicule for his long hair, didn't pay it much mind and kept driving.

Relief didn't wash over me immediately. It was delayed. I couldn't process it. Did that really happen?

Twenty or thirty miles down the road after I gained some composure, and confidence that Paul wasn't following us to an isolated area to attack, I told my dad who we had encountered.

"You won't believe who was at that gas station," I blurted out to Dad.

He turned down the music, not quite understanding.

"Paul," I said.

Dad isn't one for outward reactions, ever, but I could tell this shook him. He fell silent, truly at a loss for words. He asked me to clarify, as if he hadn't quite heard me right, asking me to repeat the story.

He was quiet, but I could feel the urge to turn the car around, yet he didn't. He kept driving.

When the divorce first happened, and Paul was making his threats, my dad's aunt back in Alabama reminded him that, "If you go to jail for what you do to Paul, who's gonna take care of those kids?"

I imagine that conversation replayed in his mind that day.

But the road stretched on, and as we left that chapter behind, I found myself in a place that would offer me something I've only recently begun to understand the importance of: stability.

Those days in Rapid City with Dad are among my most cherished memories.

During that period in my life, as a freshman in high school, I finally experienced having a full-time dad. I experienced a sense of structure and security; I knew what to expect, and I was safe and cared for.

The townhouse at 3423 Idlewild Court was a nice place to live, offering comfort and peace of mind. It wasn't calm and loving one day, then a party house with kindling ready to ignite the next. It was consistently peaceful—a steady, quiet rhythm that didn't change.

We settled into a routine. He picked me up from school on time every day and dropped me off at home before returning to work. I would watch the *Steve Wilkos Show* and indulge in a quarter sleeve of Nutter Butters and a glass of milk.

I'd wait for Dad to get home at 5:30 p.m., and each night we'd eat supper together, each with our own cold bottle of Henry Weinhard's Gourmet Root Beer.

I didn't care to make many friends, and school at Stevens High was daunting with the larger class sizes and faster pace compared to Goodland. I was completely out of my element, oblivious to the traditions, inside jokes, and rhythm of the life that everyone else seemed to know by heart.

Dad had no interest in making friends either and even less in finding a partner. To this day, he hasn't been on a date or pursued any romantic relationships since the divorce.

Every Saturday, we'd walk to the basketball court to play horse before the sun got too hot, then have lunch at The Golden Phoenix, followed by a walk in the woods and a trip to the grocery store. My deep-seated car anxiety disappeared when I was riding with him. I was comfortable. A small gesture like not smoking in the car made more of a difference than he probably realized. His car smelled brand new, no matter how many years he'd had it. And I don't only mean it was clean. It really smelled like a brand-new car fresh off of the lot.

Life was simple, yet unbelievably good. We enjoyed getting to know each other. My dad is a very stoic person, but there were signals how much he loved and cared. Reflecting on it today brings me to tears, realizing how much it meant to me then and now.

There were moments when Dad would do his best to show me how positive it would be for me to stay with him, rather than returning to Goodland. I didn't tell him what was really going on, but he knew. He tried to hold his tongue, not wanting to speak poorly of my mom in front of me, but I could tell he was torn, feeling in his heart that I would go back. He knew about the drinking, the drugs, and the partying, but if he had known everything else, I'm not sure what would have happened.

As the barriers choking my soul began to loosen, I started doing things a kid should do again, like begging for things at the store.

When we visited a music store in downtown Rapid City, I told him I would become the next Neil Peart if he bought me a drum set. And to my shock, he did.

That didn't really pan out, but playing the drums in his basement was pure magic for me.

We spent a lot of our time together walking in the woods. It wasn't *hiking*. Dad didn't want to chat or socialize; it was a spiritual practice. He called it his church. It was a place of quiet, where the stillness of the trees invited a deeper connection to what felt real and ancient. I'd never seen him more at peace than in those moments. Even when we were kids, there was a part of him that needed to reconnect with the Earth.

When we weren't in the woods, Dad showed me his favorite movies and TV shows. He was into Jet Li films: *Romeo Must Die, Unleashed,* and *Once Upon a Time in China.* And then there were the classic TV shows, like *Kung Fu* with David Carradine. Dad would pause to make sure I understood the wisdom.

One night, we watched *Friday,* and Dad gave me a warning: "I probably shouldn't let you watch this." But he did. I found that hilarious because the real life I'd been exposed to was much worse than anything I was seeing on screen.

We visited Mount Rushmore and the unfinished Crazy Horse statue, both unsettling in their own way, to be honest. We also drove to the water park in Hot Springs, South Dakota. I could see the effort Dad was making to step out of his comfort zone for me.

While I lived in Rapid City, Mom and I kept a good relationship, speaking a few times a week. She often talked about trying to get back on her feet. She left Paul and Goodland behind for a while, working on a farm in Colorado.

When we talked, her voice carried the warmth of the old mom. The simple, sweet, loving one I had cherished.

"I sure do miss you!" She would tell me.

I finished my freshman year in South Dakota, and after Dad and I drove to Seattle to visit Johnathan and Josh. Those long drives across the country are some of my favorite memories with him. He was so intentional about it: up early, starting the day with a quick continental breakfast, getting on the road as the sun came up, and without fail, playing Rush as the first music of the morning. But only after turning down the radio to listen for any strange sounds from the car.

We'd drive for a few hours, cycling through his classic collection of CDs: Yes, Cat Stevens, The Allman Brothers, Jimi Hendrix, and of course, the entire Rush discography. Then we would stop for lunch at a restaurant, a privilege to the poverty-stricken kid inside me.

Around 5:00 p.m. or so, we'd arrive at our destination for the night, stop at a gas station to pick up two big beers for Dad, unload at the hotel, and head out for dinner nearby. After, I'd beg to go to the pool, and Dad usually obliged, sitting off to the side with a book while I swam.

We started this particular drive cutting through the rugged terrain of western South Dakota, then into the corner of northeastern Wyoming and across Montana. The wide, open plains gradually gave way to the Rocky Mountains, their jagged peaks and deep valleys cutting through the land, with winding rivers and lakes scattered across the state.

By the time we hit Eastern Washington, the endless stretches of flat land and the familiar small-town rhythm hit way too close to home. It was as if I had never left Goodland.

When we crossed the Cascade Mountains, everything changed. Towering pine trees, what seemed like billions of them, completely covered the land. The air grew cooler, crisper, and refreshing. When we reached North Bend, the sight of Mount Si looming over the town wasn't anything like I'd ever seen before.

The rest of the drive was as beautiful as it was harrowing. I'll never get used to the steep drops in elevation, especially with traffic, rain, and the speed of the interstate.

As we approached Seattle, I was chomping at the bit to see my brothers, nervous and excited, determined to make the most of our time together. I'd also grown up a lot since I'd seen them last and I was eager to show them who I was now.

And I did cherish every second despite it feeling surreal. These people I'd spent so long thinking about were finally around me again.

I was happy.

The only sobering thought was that our time together was fleeting.

We lacked the emotional maturity to discuss everything that had happened, but existing in each other's presence, doing ordinary things, was healing enough. I watched closely, taking in their behaviors, attire, and interests, completely savoring everything.

We visited Josh's house in Shoreline, and he and Johnathan showed us around the city. I remember visiting Carkeek Park and walking along the beach, finding long, skinny stalks of bull kelp and other sea anemones washed up on the shore. I had no idea what they were, and they truly seemed alien.

I was soaking in everything happening around me, yet inside, I wrestled with a decision I knew none of them would agree with. A choice that would once again drive a wedge between us, both in distance and emotion.

After the trip, despite my dad's reluctance and influence, I decided to move back to Goodland.

This time, it wasn't Mom's threats or promises that drew me home. I just missed her, Grandma, Kelly, and Chris.

Telling my dad sucked. I could see the frustration in his eyes. He didn't understand. No matter how often he tried to explain why it was the wrong decision, I didn't budge.

When I told Mom, her excitement said it all. It was like she'd won the lottery. Her happiness radiated, and without hesitation, she started planning her trip up to get me.

The day I left, Dad had to work. He'd been quieter than usual in the days leading up to it, I'm sure conflicted, but that final day, with butterflies churning in my stomach, I gave him a hug goodbye. His hug was strong, it always was, but this time especially, I didn't want to let go.

I wanted both. I wanted my mom *and* my dad. Was that so much to ask?

I cried, like usual, but Dad was strong, at least in front of me. He gave me one last look before heading off to work, letting me go with a wave.

Mom came to Rapid City to pick me up, which in itself was a feat. The cars she owned couldn't reliably make it outside of Goodland, let alone across multiple state lines, but she gave it a shot. She did end up breaking down on the way up, but found a shop, got the car fixed, and made it back on the road and eventually to Idlewild Ct.

A calm settled in me the moment I saw her again. The love of my mother was exactly what I'd been craving.

We stayed in a rundown motel that night in an unfamiliar part of Rapid City, sitting together and talking, simply enjoying each other's company. I showed her the latest in technology, my iPod, and all of the Rush songs I could fit on it.

CHAPTER EIGHTEEN

Do I Tear It All Down?

Mom spending time away from Paul played a big part in my decision to return. So, on the ride to Goodland, when I found out they were together again, I was upset, but not surprised. It did suck that he ended up with the second key to the apartment.

Mom was now living in an apartment at 415 W 3rd Street, the same low-income complex where Chris lived. When Dad and I watched *Friday* not long after finding out she'd moved so close to Chris, I imagined us having neighborhood adventures like Craig and Smokey. And we did. Along with Kelly, we had a blast together, being kids, and our brotherhood helped distract me from the chaos at home.

Even though we were still incredibly poor, we managed to get by. Mom took on odd jobs, like shoveling snow at the old folks' home, often with me by her side. In fact, we loved working side by side. Whether it was in the kitchen at the bowling alley or waiting tables at the Buffalo Inn, jobs I was far too young to be doing, even as her tagalong.

She was a paradox. She spent recklessly on her addiction, yet worked tirelessly to scrape by on the essentials. At times, her resilient side would emerge, for example when she pursued and graduated with a business degree at the vo-tech. Throughout my childhood, she did nice and thoughtful things for me, but it was a confusing back-and-forth. The good moments were overshadowed by the bad memories and the constant sense that things would inevitably turn dark again.

As expected, the chaos quickly returned.

One Friday after school, Kelly and I walked to my apartment. We had plans to head to his girlfriend's house that night.

When we got to the apartment and tried to open the door, it was locked. Knowing what was ahead, I began to panic. It was winter, with snow on the ground, and we were stuck outside. Chris and his family were away for the weekend, as was my Grandma, leaving us shit out of luck.

Kelly often stayed the night with me. When he didn't, he stayed with Chris. His family lived thirty miles out in the country, and they often preferred that he stayed with friends. Most of the time, he did too.

With nowhere else to turn, Kelly asked his girlfriend if we could stay the night. Her parents weren't happy about it, I'm sure my family's reputation didn't help, but seeing the desperate situation we were in, they allowed us to sleep on their couch.

I was completely embarrassed; I tried as hard as I could to hide my problems, hoping to avoid having to talk about them or be seen as less than, but that night shattered those efforts. I couldn't even appreciate the shelter, constantly checking my TracFone for any sign of life from my mom. But she didn't show up that night and she never called. The next evening, Mom and Paul returned without any explanation of where she had been or why she hadn't come home.

Not long after, we moved to 417 E 8th Street, a modest, 768-square-foot little white house near Gulick Park. By then, my hope for anything had all but vanished.

She put in the effort to find and secure this place and was thrilled to show it to me, but I didn't realize how much my lack of enthusiasm was affecting her until Kelly pointed it out to me. I hated what I had done immediately and tried to reassure her that I was happy and excited about the place, but even now, a decade later, I still feel guilty about that moment.

I'm not sure why, but strange characters frequented that house more than any other place we'd lived since 240 Walnut. Paul was in and out of the house regularly as well. The adult from the Fourth of July incident years ago now had a son, living in town, probably in his late twenties. He was friendly to me, insisting on tuning my old guitar, or encouraging me to ride on his moped.

One day, I was outside playing catch with Kelly in the front yard when a man showed up looking for my mom. She was inside, and as he walked in, I heard him shout, "Patty! Let's hit that crack rock."

It was a small moment that severely cracked the fragile bubble I had tried so hard to maintain. Deep down, I knew what they were doing, but I had hidden myself from it as much as they had hidden it from me.

I was about fifteen years old and was now old enough to drive in Kansas when Paul asked me for a ride. Just me and him. It wasn't the kind of thing we ever did, but he insisted.

As I drove him to his new job working overnight at the big-box store in town, he retold the story of the three men who broke in and tried to kill him when he lived in Texas. The same brutal attack that left him with more than thirty stab wounds down his chest, a scar he often displayed.

I wasn't sure if what he told me next was true or if he wanted to scare me, but he described how he got revenge on each of them down by a riverbank, how he "blew him away," mimicking the motion of pulling a trigger.

A chill ran through me. I was frozen, unsure of what to say or what he meant by telling me that. I dropped him off at work, neither of us speaking for the rest of the ride or when we parted.

Despite him staying with us most of the time, Paul had recently gotten his hands on a broken-down house that he planned to fix up. My mom and I were helping him clean out the unfinished cellar, filled with dirt and cobwebs.

We went up and down those broken stairs, back and forth, carrying boxes out, but despite my efforts to help, Mom was especially harsh that day.

A few hours later, a new friend, Chase, came to hang out as we'd previously planned. As day faded into night, Mom became unhinged to a level even I hadn't seen before. I'd witnessed her transformation into someone distant and glossed over before, but tonight was worse. She wasn't there. Whoever was there was cruel, completely unconcerned about where I would sleep that night, as she settled herself in front of Paul's television. I didn't have a bed there, and she wasn't letting me go home to 417 E 8th, nor would she allow me to go to my grandma's.

Her words stopped making sense and her anger simmered. My emotions swung wildly, from indignation at this treatment, to fear for her health, asking if she was okay, only to be lashed out at again.

I hit my breaking point, so Chase and I left on foot. I broke down completely in front of my new friend while we walked the streets of Goodland that night thinking about what to do. We covered a lot of ground that night. Past the water tower on Kansas Avenue, over the bricks of Main Street, and by North School, right across from 240 Walnut.

I remember Chase looking melancholy, saying, "This is why I treat people like they might be having the worst day of their life."

Staring up at the sky, I was unsure of what to do. I had tried everything. One idea crossed my mind and wouldn't let go for hours: calling the cops to report my mom.

I gave it serious thought, considering all the consequences if I followed through. I was preparing to face the truth and stop deceiving myself about what was happening, but I wasn't sure what the police would actually do if I called. Whatever they did, I knew that it would be the end of our relationship.

Still, I was tempted to do it. I was worn down. I talked it out with Chase, and dialed 911 ready to tear everything down.

But I never hit that call button. I didn't trust myself. A small part of me wondered if I was wrong. I wanted to be wrong. But most of all, I just loved my mom too much and wasn't ready to say goodbye.

So I erased the 911 from my dial. We went inside Paul's house and Mom was as cracked out as I had ever seen her, now unresponsive in front of the TV. I went inside, grabbed her keys, and Chase and I returned to my house for the night.

CHAPTER NINETEEN

Basketball Date

The summer before my senior year of high school was nothing short of chaotic.

Paul had long since abandoned his restoration project and moved into the basement of our house at 417 E 8th Street, much to my dismay. It marked yet another chapter in the toxic, nearly decade-long cycle between him and Mom.

Now, Paul seemed focused on dating, or using, as many women as he could right in front of Mom's face. He'd be picked up by a random woman, disappear for days, and reappear like the grim reaper, slinking back into the basement. Mom's anger and hurt boiled beneath the surface. They lived to provoke each other, each seeking the reaction that would cut the deepest.

Paul had been keeping a gun in the house, usually out in the open near the living room door. But once things between him and Mom turned this time, he quietly moved it to the basement, out of sight. During their arguments, he'd throw out dark threats about the gun, but Mom stood her ground, unshaken.

At the start of summer 2010, I started getting attention from a girl that I was surprised to have noticed me.

We met at Steever Water Park, our local pool, started texting, and soon enough, she started driving to my place. We'd sit in her car, talking and kissing. The thrill of it all was electrifying. Eager to keep the momentum going, I set up a date to shoot basketball at North School, across the street from the start of our story, 240 Walnut.

Everything was falling into place perfectly. I was actually hitting a few shots and our flirting flowed effortlessly, with eye contact that neither of us wanted to break. I couldn't stop thinking about how great it all was and how much I didn't want it to end.

In my pocket, my phone started vibrating. Mom was calling. I was having such a great time that I ignored it, but she called again right away. I didn't want to answer; I was completely absorbed in the moment and didn't want her to ruin it. But she kept calling.

When I finally picked up, she was frantic, telling me that Paul had brought a woman downstairs. She demanded that I come home immediately to help her. Help with what? I had no idea. But she begged, pleaded, and threatened both herself and me if I didn't return right away.

I was furious. I had momentarily escaped a shit situation, finding simple relief in young lust that boosted my low confidence. But just as quickly, it was ripped away, forcing me into a problem I should have never been involved in.

This girl came from a completely different world than mine. Her parents were respected members of the community, with a strong reputation, and I knew they wouldn't want their daughter involved with me. In a previous fling, I'd heard from another girl that her parents saw me as someone with no future.

I tried to hide that part of my life when I was with her, hoping those problems didn't define me. But deep down, I knew it was over after this.

When I got home, Mom kept desperately repeating the same frantic lines:

"He has a girl downstairs,"

"Call the cops!"

"Make him get out! Do something!"

She was crying harder and more hysterically than I had seen in years, but even so, this was different. With blood boiling, I finally stood up for myself. The words came before I could stop them. I told her that what he was doing wasn't illegal and reminded her that she was the one who had let him into the house.

She hated hearing that from me.

The hurt in her eyes was palpable, her face swollen with betrayal. She raised her fist as if she were going to punch me and that's when I walked away.

It hurts me deeply to remember that day. She was lost, flailing in a storm of emotions. I had exhausted every avenue, every desperate attempt to reach her, to pull her from the edge for the last nine years.

The image of her, broken and at her wits' end, haunts and lingers in the corners of my mind. Today it brings a heaviness to my chest that I can't shake. Her agony was mine too, and the echoes of it reverberate within me, a constant reminder of the bond we share. No matter how fractured.

I didn't want to stand up to my mom, partly because I was manipulated, but also because I didn't want the memory of acting mean toward her burned in my mind.

Not long after that incident, maybe a few days later, the tension between Paul and my mom escalated even further.

I drove home with Kelly and Chris in tow one afternoon, and I parked on the street where I normally would. Mom freaked out, yelling at me from the door that I had to park on the side of the house. I didn't think much of it and moved the car.

Later, Paul came to the house in a full-blown rage. He whipped open the back door, baseball bat in hand, and cocked back to swing when he saw me standing alone in the kitchen. He screamed, "Did you park the fucking car there?"

I replied, "I had to."

He started backing me into a corner as Kelly stormed into the kitchen. He saw Paul with the bat cocked, grabbed him by the throat, and slammed him hard against the cabinets.

Chris ran into the kitchen, poised and ready. Kelly let go of Paul, who, realizing for the first time he was outnumbered, retreated downstairs to his gun.

We all got out of the house and I called 911, pausing briefly as the thought of what might happen when he got out of jail crossed my mind before finally following through.

The police arrived quickly and entered the house with their weapons in hand. Minutes later, I watched as they led Paul out of the house in handcuffs, without incident.

Part of me was relieved to *finally* see him in handcuffs, a sight I'd longed for, but another part knew a line had been crossed, and I'd have to face his reaction.

Later that same night, we heard the back door creak open and footsteps walking down to the basement, followed by the door slamming shut.

Paul was here.

I knew he had other places to go. He bragged about them to put Mom down, but he chose to return that night, I believe, to taunt us. To reignite the pain in our hearts.

CHAPTER TWENTY

Goodbye Goodland

In 2011, my senior year was underway, and with it the changes kept coming. After injuries ended my flailing high school football career, I wanted to stay connected with the team, especially with Kelly and Chris, who were the star players. So, I reached out to the *Goodland Star-News* and asked if I could cover the football team for them. After submitting a test article to the editor, Tom Betz, I was hired.

The sports director at the local radio station, Jay Sanderson, came across some of my articles and invited me to join his morning radio show for an interview. We hit it off, and he added me as a daily cohost. He also gave me opportunities to do color commentary for football games, be the in-studio host for basketball games, and called play-by-play for volleyball and state championship wrestling. When he was hired to do play-by-play for the state football championship on TV in Wichita, he took me along as the sideline reporter.

I had the opportunity to get to know town legends Curtis Duncan, the voice of Goodland, and Ron Rempe, the encyclopedia of music for Northwest Kansas.

For the first time in my life, I believed I was good at something.

Before this, I never saw myself as smart or attractive, and I definitely wasn't rich. I'd never been to a dentist and hated how my teeth looked. With the lingering cigarette smell, I figured I wasn't all that desirable of a person to be around.

So, this new sense of confidence meant everything to me. I wasn't doing it to be popular or impress others; I needed to prove it to myself.

A decade later, when I returned to visit Goodland, my Uncle Rod confided that he had worried about me growing up because of how weird and different I was. He hoped I would eventually come around, but instead, he said, "Everyone came around to you."

That touched me deeply. I don't expect most people to understand me on a surface level, and certainly not on a deeper level, so his words meant the world.

I finished high school on quite a high. I was still dealing with the same issues at home, but I was busier with school, the radio, and girls.

Kelly stayed with me almost every night, and his presence kept the unease with Paul at bay.

That same year, I discovered the emotional release that came with drinking. The shift in feeling, the altered state, brought both a strange clarity and a precarious realization: *Oh. This is how people manage to get through life.* If I hadn't witnessed the destruction it could cause firsthand, this path might have turned out far worse than it did.

There were nights when my friends and I ended up drinking with Mom and Paul. Some of the guys knew him as Kalyn's dad, and, somehow, he was starting to be accepted as part of the community. It made me sick, but after years of struggling and fighting battles I couldn't win, I bit my tongue and tried to enjoy partying with my friends. I didn't invite Paul, but he found a way to weasel himself in, playing a character I knew to be bullshit.

Around the same time, I started reconnecting with my brother Josh on Facebook. We would message each other catching up, and talk about the possibility of me moving to Seattle to live with him once I finished high school.

I had looked forward to it ever since they left. It was a reason to keep pushing through. But the thought of living in the same city as them again seemed like a fantasy. But I knew I needed to get to Seattle, to be with my brothers, and finally get away from this chaos.

Yet almost everyone around me was pressuring me to stay in Goodland. As they saw it, things were finally starting to go well for me. I had been informally promised the position of sports director at the radio station, a wild job for an 18-year-old, while I attended Colby Community College's broadcasting program. To most people, it seemed to be a no-brainer.

For example, Uncle Troy commented on a post of mine on social media:

Stay on track with your school plans and your career. I want to see your ass on Fox Sports, calling the Cowboys game and making a shitload of money. I know you will be an excellent sportscaster or sports director. Your sports knowledge is nothing short of amazing. You can write your own ticket to whatever you want to do. Put in the hard work now and life will become easier and easier in no time at all. Your Mom, Pam and I and Grandma are so damn proud of you, we could bust. I know Grandpa is looking down at you with the biggest smile on his face. Make your Grandpa proud. We all love you and just want the best for you......... Go Cowboys!!!!!!!!

A different family member took me on a drive and told me "Get your work in now with college and then go have fun with your brothers later."

I knew they were saying it out of love, wanting the best for me, but it was hard not to hear the subtext: This is your only shot. You've had a rough life and have no future prospects, so this is it. Don't screw it up.

I was at a crossroads.

Some days, driving to school from a great morning on the radio, I couldn't imagine giving it up. I had taken my love for football and turned it into a dream job.

My extended family was so proud that I'd finally made a name for myself, that I had a future. And the people in Goodland, the ones who had questioned me and who I was my entire life for being different, were suddenly paying me positive attention. The ones who had issues with my long hair, my painted nails, my women's jeans. The ones who couldn't understand why I wasn't religious, why I didn't agree with how they treated their farm animals, why I supported gay people and marriage equality. Those same people were now supporting me, stopping to talk at restaurants, bringing up things I'd said on the radio that morning or the day before. Suddenly I was someone worth knowing.

I could articulate all the reasons why staying made sense better than I could for leaving, but that was only because I was young and had closed off so much of my mind for my own safety. I couldn't put the words together to explain it to anyone, but deep down, I knew what I needed to do.

I resented what they were telling me. I understood what they were doing, after seeing me struggle so much and finally get a good opportunity. But to me, it only confirmed that they didn't truly understand what would fix the pain in my heart.

It was never going to be a fucking job.

I couldn't explain why to them at the time, but throwing this opportunity right in the garbage was absolutely the right thing for me to do. I couldn't undo or fix what my mom had done to me, but I could fix the separation from my brothers.

For as long as I can remember, I've carried a deep-seated need to please the people I care about, driven by an almost desperate anxiety about letting them down. But like an old, battered tree in windy-ass, miserable Kansas, I stood strong, and set my date to leave, permanently, at the end of June.

I signed off from the radio for the final time and wrote my final article for the Goodland Star-News. With a heavy heart, I stopped by 206 Broadway to say a tearful goodbye to Grandma and Nathan, packed up all my belongings, and got ready for Dad to pick me up and drive me to Seattle.

On my last day in Goodland, Kelly and Chris, who were lifeguards, spent part of the day with me swimming after hours at the pool. I spent some time with Mom, but Paul was around, so it wasn't what I'd hoped it would be.

Mom looked defeated. I had seen her cry more than anyone else in the world, and I know I've said it before, but this was a particularly sad cry. I don't know if it was because I was leaving and she wouldn't have her boy there, or if she realized what she had put me through the last nine years, and that it never got better.

The air was thick with emotion as I loaded my bags into Kelly's car, preparing for him to drive me to meet my dad at the hotel. The tension was heart-wrenching and heavy. Mom was on the verge of either tears or shouting at any moment. She knew this was the end. The story had been written and there was no going back.

Mom and I had been through hell together, but I still loved her, and it hurt me then, and hurts me today, to know how sad she was that day.

With 4 Non Blondes' *What's Up?* ringing in my ears from her stereo, I gave her one last hug before getting into Kelly's car. Chris was there waiting, and they drove me to Dad's hotel.

These two guys had made such a difference in my life and loved me so fully. They had become my brothers.

CHAPTER TWENTY-ONE

Seattle

As we made our way west, I stared out the window of Dad's car, pinching my skin to see if I could feel it, double-checking that it was real. I glanced at Dad; he was as calm as ever, round black sunglasses on, his gaze fixed on the road. His car smelled brand new, like always. I imagined what life would be like in Seattle and what Mom's life would be like without me.

This was a pivotal stage in my life, and similar to most 18-year-olds, I was overly confident.

I'd spent almost my entire life in one small town in Northwest Kansas and was now moving nearly 1,500 miles away to a city that was several hundred times larger. My dad, now living in South Dakota, wouldn't be staying long, only dropping me off at Josh's studio apartment at 4755 22nd Ave NE in the University District.

Johnathan lived in the Central District, which, to me at the time, might as well have been on a different planet. But in reality, it was a short metro bus ride away, so he was around, too.

With a cot and whatever I could fit into a suitcase, I began my new life in the corner of Josh's apartment.

The feeling of having my brothers around again stirred the heavy emotions I thought I'd buried. Even though what we were doing was simple, it felt sacred. It grounded me and allowed me to build a foundation for the rest of my life.

I was finally correcting one of my long-standing injustices. So that's what we did, we picked up where we had left off nine years earlier. We got to know each other again, slowly but surely, by spending time together and reclaiming the remnants of our childhoods. Without Paul.

After they left in 2002, I was reminded how they traveled the country by car with Dad, moving from jobsite to jobsite until they landed in Issaquah, Washington. I remembered how they had to start completely over with nothing, not even the savings Dad had built up all those years. The child support taken from his paycheck hit them hard too.

It wasn't easy for any of them. Dad was trying to figure out how to be "Mr. Mom," as he put it, and Johnathan and Josh were facing the reality of having been pushed out of their old life by their mom and starting over thousands of miles away as teenagers. Around the time Johnathan finished high school, Dad's job took him to Rapid City, South Dakota. Johnathan went with him but only stayed a year before returning to Seattle.

Josh, at seventeen and with a school year left, chose to stay behind. His band, Antlers, was taking off, and moreover, Seattle had become his home.

While this was a therapeutic period for me, my mind was spinning. I believed that leaving the situation with Paul and my mom would improve my emotional and mental state, but instead, it worsened.

Behind the scenes, out of view of my everyday mind, my brain began to decompress after all that had happened in the last nine years. I carried the pain and hurt from what had happened, but was walled off from really processing it. I just didn't have the tools.

All of that stacked on the pressure of being eighteen and thinking that I had to have my life figured out, made me into a boiling tea kettle with no way to let out the steam.

There were days early on in Seattle when I made serious plans to escape and live at a monastery in rural Washington, tapping out of regular life. In reality, I could barely navigate the U-District, so that plan was always far-fetched.

Spending time with my brothers was my priority, so I passed on pursuing radio jobs and took a retail position in the nearby University Village mall at a jeans store. It was a job that took the right amount of attention.

I was making minimum wage, but living was easy. I noticed it was a lot easier to be poor in Seattle than in Goodland. There was an infrastructure for it—buses, bigger food banks, and thrift stores that people weren't ashamed to use. It was strange seeing the popular crowd shopping at thrift stores. In Goodland, it would have been a permanent stain on your reputation, and Mom and I had already done it with our heads down.

Overall, the first few years living in Seattle with my brothers nourished my soul in ways I never expected. It was a powerful boost to my confidence to have made it happen, to finally start healing one of the wounds that Paul and Mom had left on my heart.

But it took time and effort to rebuild the relationship with my brothers. At first, we didn't know where to start. But the important part was already taken care of: we were together.

With Josh and I living together, he took me under his wing, helping me evolve from a small-town kid into someone who loved the possibilities of the city. He introduced me to his favorite food spots in the U-District: Kikus, Nasai Teriyaki, Taste of India, and Aladdin's. The walks to and from the restaurant, often through Ravenna Park, a half-mile wooded ravine close to our apartment, were just as important. As Neil Peart once wrote, "The point of a journey is not to arrive."

He also showed me how to navigate the bus system, which was one of the most mind-boggling things I'd had to figure out since moving. Everything moved so fast. People moving in every direction, the constant shuffle of stops, the endless possibilities of where I could end up if I wasn't paying attention. I remember first stepping off the bus near the 3rd and Pine McDonald's, the city's most well-known landing spot for people who had fallen on hard times. A crossroads of addiction and survival.

We bussed all over the city, jumping from one party to another, chasing whatever adventure came up that night. We also spent a lot of our days at home. We didn't have cable, and it was too early for streaming, but we had the DVD version of Led Zeppelin's Earl's Court 1975 performance. We wore that disc out, playing it almost constantly, awestruck by Robert Plant's presence and John Bonham's rumbling fills.

Johnathan and I had to work harder to rebuild our bond. It started with me taking the bus to the Central District, meeting him at the park near his house for hours of one-on-one basketball. Later, we moved inside to the Meredith Mathews East Madison YMCA, then took it to higher levels, like full court one-on-one, first to 100.

Johnathan was a deadeye shooter. If you gave him space at the arc, he'd bury you. I relied on my speed, blowing past him on defense, only to miss the open layup. But it wasn't really about the game.

I'd drop into my defensive stance, watching him, and the weight of it would hit me. After years of separation, I was a kid playing basketball with my brother again, back where we started.

The three of us started going to shows, watching their friends' bands play in small, grimy venues. It was fascinating to take in the social dynamics. From the performers to the crowd, to strangers interacting between sets at the front of the venue. Johnathan knew everyone. Most of them knew Josh too, especially from his performing days. The music was raw, loud, and progressive, exposing me to sounds I hadn't heard before.

A lot of nights, we'd end up at Cal Anderson Park or Linda's Tavern on Capitol Hill. Linda's was our favorite stop. A classic Seattle dive bar with a great back patio. I didn't realize its history until later, reading that it was once called the "grunge Cheers."

Seattle urban legend says Linda's was the last place Kurt Cobain was seen alive, with grainy pictures floating online of the booth they believe he sat in that night. He was a regular there, along with some of the guys from Soundgarden and Pearl Jam. When news of his death broke, a huge part of the city's music community gathered at Linda's to mourn, while news cameras sat outside, kept out by the owners.

During the summer of 2012, Josh and I made our way to Goodland, a place he hadn't visited in what seemed like forever. As the trip loomed closer, my body had a visceral response. My appetite vanished and sleep became irregular at best.

At first, I blamed it on the anxiety of flying, but I've come to realize that I really enjoy flying. Flying feels safer than riding in a car. This reaction became all too familiar, that gnawing dread that surfaced whenever a visit to Goodland was on the calendar.

When we arrived, Mom was there to greet us at the airport, and we spent some truly meaningful time together. It was clear she took pride in working hard and buying herself a car reliable enough to get her to Denver, and in having her boys with her, even if it was temporary.

Just existing near her gave me a feeling nothing else could. Her love was un-matched when it wasn't drowned out. For once, there was no pressure, no expec-tation that I would stay.

The energy was thick that first night home, charged in a way I couldn't ignore. Josh and I stayed with Grandma, a deliberate move to avoid Paul. Summer was in town too, and Josh was fired up to be back in Goodland as an adult, ready to grab the bull by the horns.

The hug I got from Grandma put me at ease in a way nothing had in the year I was gone. Despite that, I had a much harder time acclimating. I could feel the weight of the changes I'd already been through by getting away from the chaos. For the first time, I truly understood the sentiment: you can never go home. It had changed. *I had changed.* I was more reserved, less excitable. I ran into old friends, and I could see it in their faces: my energy had shifted. Not in a bad way, but noticeable.

When we all got together and went out to eat, it should have been perfect. But my nerves were shot. I couldn't eat. Everything I had left behind had crept back in. Pressing against my chest, tightening in my stomach and flooding my mind.

The trip went by too fast. Before I knew it, we were headed west on I-70 to Denver International Airport. But in those moments, especially, Josh and I were healing. Reconnecting as brothers through new experiences, finding solace in the bond that time and distance couldn't break.

CHAPTER TWENTY-TWO

She's Gone

Later in 2012, Mom was diagnosed with lung cancer.

My uncle Troy got in contact with me, insisting that we all needed to have a group call. Him, my brothers, me, and Mom. During that call, he explained that our mom had been diagnosed with cancer, relaying that she didn't have the heart to tell us herself. Troy tried to reassure us, saying it wasn't that serious and that she would be fine.

My gut told me he was lying. She would not be fine. All of my emotions swirled. I worried about her. I felt for my brothers. I was furious with the universe. I tried to avoid thinking about how I felt because, just below the surface, I was completely devastated. I started to close up inside, the way a city boards its windows before a hurricane.

Mom and I had stayed in close contact since I left Goodland. We talked on the phone at least once every few days and exchanged texts daily. We never discussed the past, especially the bad things that happened when I lived with her. Instead, we focused on supporting each other, acting as the ultimate friends, rooting for each other and showing up when one of us was feeling down.

She came to visit later that year and stayed with Josh and me. By then, we had moved upstairs to a two-bedroom apartment in the same building at 4755 22nd Ave.

Mom had recently moved out of Goodland and headed west for Kiowa, Colorado, to live with her cousin Terri and husband Ken. The old Mom was back, with no trace of Paul around to wreck everything.

During this trip, her relationship with my brothers also improved immensely. Understandably, they hadn't been as quick to forgive her, but over the years they started speaking again. Now more than ever, she was on a mission to be our mom again. She stocked the fridge, cooked meals like she used to, and stepped into the role of mother that we'd been missing while on our own in Seattle.

Most of all, she seemed genuinely at peace. She talked to strangers effortlessly as we wandered around the U-District and actually stopped to smell the flowers. We'd sit together and talk, usually laughing about whatever came to mind, or the episode of *Trailer Park Boys* we were watching, until it was time to go to bed. She would get set up in my room as I got comfortable on the couch. We'd meet at my bedroom door, and she would give me a hug and kiss goodnight, telling me 'sweet dreams' for old times' sake.

She never talked about having fear of her diagnosis, she played it off as nothing. Neither of us wanted our conversations to get too heavy, but one evening, I did ask her if she had any bucket list items. She told me it had been a dream of hers to ride on a big ship in the ocean. That was the first time I had heard that from her before, but it made sense. She was a Kansas girl after all.

After a few weeks, it was time for Mom to head home to Colorado. We rode the light rail together to the airport and said our goodbyes by the security line at SeaTac airport. Neither of us liked goodbyes, but this trip had been such a success that this one didn't sting quite as much.

A few months later, on February 8th, 2013, after a lifelong battle with health complications from his spinal injury, Uncle Troy passed away at age 48.

I couldn't imagine what it was like for Mom to lose her brother. Despite the hard times between them when Troy took me in, they had grown close again, which she told me how much that meant to her.

A few weeks after his death, I started coordinating with Mom to plan a trip home to see her. We were waiting for her boss to approve her time off request, and I was anxious all day, ready for the green light to buy the plane tickets. All I wanted was to buy those tickets and confirm that I was going home to see my mom.

That morning, my phone was eerily silent. So much so that I called my workplace to make sure my phone was functioning. When they answered, I hung up before saying anything, realizing the problem wasn't on my end.

Hours later, I finally got the reply I had been waiting for from Mom.

"I'm sure he will let me off. Go ahead and buy them :)"

Boom. It probably wasn't ten minutes after my phone vibrated with that text when I punched my ticket and made it official. Finally, I could move on and enjoy the rest of my day.

Later that night, I received a Facebook messenger notification from my cousin, Leah, Terri's daughter. The message was brief and unsettling: "Call me ASAP," with her phone number listed at the bottom.

The moment I read those words, I knew there was no going back. I couldn't unsee the message and make the problem go away. Whatever I was about to hear would change everything. I dialed the number, and the phone barely rang before a voice I hadn't heard in years answered. Leah's voice was tense, her attempt at small talk only a thin veil over the urgency of the call.

"Well, bud, I wish I had better news for you," she began, her voice heavy with the weight of what she had to say.

Leah explained that my mom and Terri happened to get off work at the same time that afternoon and were headed home in separate cars. Terri pulled out first with Mom following behind. About halfway home, Terri noticed she was no longer behind her. She assumed Mom had either forgotten something at work or stopped off to get beer. But after more time passed and Mom still hadn't arrived home, Terri's concern started to grow.

Mom had suffered a stroke and a heart attack while driving home that day.

She crashed into a ditch, but after regaining consciousness, somehow managed to drive herself out and make it the rest of the way to Terri's house. When she pulled into the driveway, she was in a panic, desperate to get inside. Terri asked if she was okay, but Mom couldn't speak.

Terri called an ambulance as Mom rushed to the bathroom to pee. She was quickly taken to the emergency room and then flown to the Denver area for life-saving care.

Before I knew it, I was in the same security line where I had last left Mom months ago, and soon on a plane to Colorado. At that moment, I was mostly numb and blank, unsure if I'd be able to stop thinking or crying once I started.

When I arrived at the airport in Denver, Terri was there waiting for me at baggage claim. I spotted her when I was coming down the escalator and managed a small smile, but she didn't return it. Instead, she shook her head and pulled me into a hug.

We drove to Breckenridge, Colorado to the hospital where Mom was. When we made our way to her floor, Terri walked ahead of me and I paused at the doorway before going in, letting her go in first.

I needed a moment.

I knew what I saw once I crossed that threshold might break my heart.

After taking that brief moment, I stepped into the room and saw my mom lying on the hospital bed. Our eyes met, and words weren't necessary. We just hugged each other and cried.

The left side of her face was drooping, and her arm hung limp, unable to move. She couldn't speak, but her eyes were still connected to her soul.

I don't recall exactly how long I stayed, maybe a week, but during that time, we moved her from the hospital to a rehab facility to help her recover from the stroke. I would lie beside her in bed, and we'd watch *Trailer Park Boys*. During the day, I'd take her outside in her wheelchair, and we'd sit at a picnic table, listening to Jimi Hendrix, her favorite song *Little Wing*, and the *Band of Gypsys* album.

She couldn't speak, but our connection was unbroken.

Outside of spending time with me, she grew increasingly frustrated during rehab sessions when they seemed to go nowhere. I saw that same defeated look in her eyes that Nathan had sometimes. She was still there, somewhere deep inside, but the connection to reach us was lost.

I remember a nurse asking my age. I told her I was 19, and that my mom was 52. Her face fell and her eyes went vacant, muttering that we were both so young. After everything I'd been through, I didn't feel that young. But now, a decade later, I'm beginning to understand.

Chris made the long drive from Goodland to visit us and show his support. Having him there held me up when I was closest to falling apart.

The day came when I had to leave Colorado and return to Seattle for work. My brothers had agreed to take over looking after Mom, and they would be on their way soon.

On that cold winter morning, I gathered every ounce of resolve I had and walked from my hotel to the rehab center one last time.

Mom and I sat together on her hospital bed, holding each other close as the day passed faster than either of us would have liked. I held her hand, though I wasn't sure she could feel it.

But the stroke, the heart attack, and the cancer hadn't taken everything. She was still my mom. That connection, the same one from before the dark days, was strong. It was the same warmth from the night all those years back when we played Mad Libs, the same unspoken, but all-powerful tether that bound us.

I hugged her as long and as hard as I could, kissed her cheek. There was nothing more familiar than the feeling of hugging her, of holding her close.

"I'll be back," I told her, fighting through tears.

I stood a few steps away from the foot of her bed. Only the two of us. It was as if the universe had given us a moment. The world was spinning around us, but in that room, we were still.

Mom looked at me, her eyes soaked with tears and overflowing with all the love in the world. I could see it. There was a pressure building in her chest, desperate to break free but locked inside.

Something important.

I think she was trying to tell me goodbye.

But her inability to speak might have been fate. Because finding or hearing those words would have been too hard anyway.

It took everything I had to walk out of that room. To willingly say goodbye. I turned back more than once, not wanting the moment to end. But when I *had* to go or miss my flight, I looked at her one last time and smiled through the tears, wanting her to know that I would be okay. And then I forced myself to put one foot in front of the other and leave her room.

It took all I had to stay upright during that walk through the snow to my hotel. The snow crunched hard beneath my feet, slick and unforgiving, while my chest burned with a searing heat. Every nerve in my body was firing in a losing battle to steady me. The weight of the moment pressed down on me.

Mom passed away a few weeks later on March 28th, 2013, only days after my brothers arrived.

Johnathan called while I was at my retail job back in Seattle, standing at the cash register. When my phone vibrated and I saw it was him, I walked off the floor and answered.

He told me, "She's gone."

I left work that day, not wanting to go home to an empty apartment. So, I wandered through Ravenna Park until I found a secluded spot deep in the trees.

My body sank to the ground, and my heart broke open. Years of holding it together, of swallowing grief and staying strong, finally shattered. The weight of it all finally overflowed. It was the kind of crying that tears through you, leaving nothing untouched.

I was baptized in my own tears. The person I was before it was now gone.

The world spun around me again, but this time, there was no stillness, it was only faster and more dizzying.

That night, my manager from my retail job, Marissa, and my new friend from work, Evan, came to check on me. They brought a case of beer, and sat with me. I probably didn't say much, but their presence meant the world to me.

I thought it was unfair that after all we had been through, I lost her. Just like that. I had the rest of my life to go, and I would never see her again. Never look her in the eyes. I hurt for my brothers and for my grandma, who had just lost her second child in 48 days.

I was mad at the universe and started to think it was personal.

I felt confused about how someone I was that close with could just be gone. I thought there must be a way she would be able to reach me.

For some reason I still don't understand, I felt relieved. Maybe it was just because she was already struggling so much physically. Maybe it was because, for so many years, I lay awake worrying about all the ways I might lose her, especially when she didn't come home.

Maybe it was because after so many years of harsh distance she had put between her and my brothers emotionally, they had finally reconciled and were in the best place they had been in years, and I didn't want that to go south.

Any relief I felt in my broken mind would soon fade with the cold reality that my mom was gone.

Late that night, my brothers came home. Their flight had already been scheduled for that evening and she died less than an hour before they were supposed to leave. Standing there afterward, they realized, 'She's not here anymore,' and left for the airport. Being together as brothers meant a lot to us before, but never like it did right then.

We traveled to Goodland for her funeral about a week later. As has become tradition, Chris was there in Denver, ready to pick us up and drive us the 200 miles home—having just made that same drive from Goodland to get us.

When we arrived at Grandma's house that night, my uncles—Rod, Tony, and Mike—were there. I'll never forget the hug Mike gave me. He was in so much pain himself, but he knew how much I was hurting too. The reality of it all began to sink in. I laid my head against his chest and cried, the scent of his shirt lingering in my memory today.

The day of her funeral, we three brothers walked there together, separate from everyone else. Despite everything, we were together again.

Bonded.

Solidified.

Ready to face this challenge together.

And we did.

When I walked in, I was holding it together, standing strong, until I saw Chris. I hugged him and fell apart in his arms. He held me and let me cry.

My brothers and I sat in the front row with Grandma and we put Mom to rest.

Watching my uncles, her brothers, alongside Kelly and Chris carry her casket struck deep within me.

I had lost my mother, but I wasn't alone.

CHAPTER TWENTY-THREE

Afterimage

The years following my mom's death were a blur.

That day of her funeral was hard, but the days that followed were difficult too. With time, her absence only grows heavier. Birthdays, hers and mine, are especially hard.

I notice her absence in the most trivial ways, like not being able to talk to her about what's happening in the world.

Losing her changed the way I viewed every relationship in my life, constantly fixating on the fact that they, too, would die, and I would never see them again. I didn't want to be close to anyone because I couldn't handle the thought of more loss. Impending doom lived in my gut.

To this day, it kills me not to have her here for the better times. I'm in such a better place now, able to help her get back on her feet, which I couldn't do back then. I didn't have the means to get her on that big ship before, but I do now. And yet, I can't.

Even though I'm not religious, I've had to hold on to the hope that I might see her again one day, anything to avoid the mind-fuck that you will never see someone you were that close to ever again after they die.

My brothers and I stuck together now more than ever, beginning to understand the weight and importance of remaining close. We didn't have the words, but we showed up for each other, becoming a solid and steady support system.

Before Mom died, Dad had landed a job in the Seattle area. It was the first time since those six months in 2007 that I had him around full-time as a dad. The feeling was almost unreal, helping to counteract the irrepressible sadness I was carrying. He'd drive down to the U-District to eat a burger with us, or we'd bus to him across Lake Washington and walk in the woods together. Some of my favorite times were loading into the car to see Rush live, a privilege I had five times. The simplicity of having him around and spending time with him was a feeling I'd wished for so long. Now, I didn't just have my brothers, I had my dad too.

Sometime in 2014, I was working on Capitol Hill, when I struck up a conversation with a regular customer, a man in his late 40s or early 50s. We had an unspoken connection. At first he never mentioned he was a therapist and I never mentioned my struggles, but the universe kept putting him in front of me. We talked about his previous life and about me writing a book for him. We met for coffee and he shared that he was a therapist. I was too poor to have ever seen a therapist, but through some miracle, he took me in as a client.

Revisiting those old wounds was agonizing, and I struggled to recover mentally after our sessions. I avoided going regularly because, on the surface, I managed to hold myself together day-by-day. Deliberately reopening those wounds was too painful and debilitating.

I had left it behind, but it hadn't left me.

The same confusion and crippling anxiety crept back in, settling in my chest. I wasn't able to communicate my problems or my feelings in other areas of my life, partly because I didn't fully understand them myself.

There were hard truths I had to confront. About myself, my mom, and everything that had happened. I needed to wade through it all to figure out who I truly am, like if my kindness was there before all of this or if it was a result of this. I'd avoided conflict and treated everyone with the same kid gloves that I used with Mom and Paul. This approach served me well throughout my life. It made me considerate, calm, and kind, qualities that are inherent to who I am. But sometimes, I question whether these traits were the result of a defense mechanism or a reflection of my true self.

I started avoiding appointments, rescheduling, falling off the map and letting myself slip out of the habit of going. I was happy to distract myself with other things. Some valuable and important, some not.

Johnathan and I kept playing basketball together, falling in love with the game as we went. We'd watch games on the best stream we could find on Reddit (that would inevitably freeze at the most important part of the game), completely immersed in the teams and storylines.

We made a trip down to Portland to see an NBA game together. We stood in the literal last row, the highest spot in the arena, but it didn't matter. It was unbelievable to be there together.

Toward the summer, Johnathan texted me and mentioned that an NBA player was hosting basketball games at the Rainier Vista Boys and Girls Club. One Saturday, we took a combination of buses and made it down to Jamal Crawford's summer pro-am for the first time.

We stood in amazement as we watched high level hoop up close and personal for the first time. We couldn't find a seat, but we were happy enough to be in the gym. After the game, I walked up to one of the star players, Tony Wroten, and gave him a high five. He casually gave me one back, accepting me in a small but meaningful way.

The pro-am became our favorite thing to do together. We'd go every weekend and talk about it all week. That went on for multiple summers, following them as they moved to a larger gym in Queen Anne. The excitement grew as bigger and bigger names started showing up—Isaiah Thomas, Blake Griffin, Kevin Durant. We'd watch Jamal's social media closely for announcements, desperate to figure out who might show up next.

Then came the announcement: Kobe Bryant would be in the building to watch live and local Seattle basketball. We dropped what we were doing and sprinted to the bus as fast as we could, desperate to get the best spot. Time refused to slow down.

But we made it, early enough to land front row seats. Kobe walked out, sunglasses on, to a thunderous roar from the fans. We were maybe twenty feet away when I let out a heartfelt "Kobe!"

Johnathan and I knew we had found a sacred place. We cherished every weekend we spent there, soaking it all in together.

Josh and I were living together, spending as much time with each other, and with Johnathan, as we could. One afternoon, Josh and I were both off work, trying to figure out what to get into. We ended up scrolling through the free section on Craigslist, probably looking for a chair or a side table for the apartment. That's when I stumbled on a post about a cat in need of a home.

The owner was moving to Australia and couldn't take the cat. Their original plan had fallen through at the last minute, leaving them scrambling. In the spirit of our usual freewheeling attitude, we decided to go for it, reflecting on all the good memories we had with the cats we grew up with. After a few emails, we walked over to the person's house.

The moment I walked through the door, a domestic shorthair brown tabby trotted toward me and flopped onto his side, inviting me to say hi. My heart lit up. The connection was instant. He was a charismatic, healthy looking young cat, aside from the layer of unbrushed dead hair clinging to his coat.

From that day on, that tabby enriched our lives to levels we didn't know were possible. He quickly became a prominent character in our lives as his personality started to show through—from jumping out of the second-floor bathroom window, to meowing at the door of other apartments in the building to beg for food, to stealing pieces of bread out of our kitchen cabinet, and leaving behind an endless trail of death from his outdoor hunting sprees. (We shouldn't have let him be an outdoor cat, but we didn't know any better.)

He was cunning and smart. He'd trick Josh and me into feeding him dinner twice, meowing with heart-wrenching desperation that made it impossible not to believe him. He knew exactly how to wake me up in the morning, down to the timing, tone, tempo, and volume of his meows just right to where I had no choice but to feed him.

He might not have arrived with that name, but he made it clear he was The Rat.

Above all, he reminded us what it meant to be loved. The warmth we had lost when Mom died. At first, he was guarded, but Josh and I were so affectionate and hands-on that he started to lean into it. When he decided it was time to sit on your lap, there wasn't a more tender animal. He'd curl up, heavy and warm, purring so hard you could feel the vibration through your legs. His slow blinks were his way of showing he trusted us. He'd fall asleep there for hours, a lot of times covering his eyes with his paws.

It was clear he loved us as much as we loved him.

Still, that time together with my brothers wasn't easy. We were processing losing our mom with so much of our lives ahead of us and so much of the past unresolved. But this time, we faced the grief and trauma together. And that made all the difference. It brought us closer than we had ever been before.

Johnathan had also moved to the apartment building at 4755 22nd Ave, into the studio apartment Josh and I had shared all those years ago. The Rat would visit Johnathan, meowing at his window until he let him in.

Basketball remained central in both of our lives. As we got better, we started taking pick-up games more seriously. Some of my favorite moments were us playing together as a team against random people. I'd drive recklessly to the rim, again no chance of hitting the layup, but I was learning to dial in my passes right to Johnathan's shooting pocket, usually in the corner where he'd drain a three.

Memorial Day weekend in 2015, Johnathan and I planned to pack the days full of basketball, taking advantage of the good weather.

That weekend, I'd also set up a date with a co-worker. We'd worked together for about six months, and I'd deliberately tried not to flirt with her. She was so pretty, clearly smart and confident. Confident in a way that makes you second-guess yourself. I figured she was expecting me to flirt, so I didn't.

Until one day, she was nice enough to give me a ride home when we realized we lived a few blocks apart. After a few rides, I asked if she wanted to get drinks that Friday night, "since we live close to each other."

I hadn't the slightest idea if she liked me or not. She was proudly stoic, but I was also proudly ambitious.

She agreed. The date went well, but by the end, I still couldn't really tell if she saw me as more than a friend. As we walked toward our apartments, mine was the first stop. I posed a question—"Do you want to meet The Rat?"—as she and everyone else in my orbit had heard plenty of stories about him. I didn't realize it at the time, but whether she liked me or not, she couldn't say no to a cat. With The Rat's help, I got a kiss to end the night, leaving no doubt that Jazmine liked me as more than a friend.

The next morning, riding high off a successful date, Johnathan and I decided to meet up at our favorite basketball court on the University of Washington campus, right off of 45th and 19th Ave.

Two other guys were already on the court, a perfect setup for two-on-two. I challenged them to a game and they accepted.

A few possessions in, I was the on-ball defender. I was feeling myself after all my recent practice, sometimes twice a day, and dating success on top of that.

I was locked in, playing aggressive, tight defense. The opponent went up for a shot, and I tracked it the whole way, leaping up, ready to send it to the next zip code. But my timing was a fraction off. I came down awkwardly, toes first.

Snap.

A hard crack echoed through my body as my ankle bones shifted and caught. I came to on my back, the pain flooding in all at once. I wailed continuously.

Johnathan said he heard it but didn't see it and didn't think the scream came from me; it didn't sound like me at all.

My foot was cranked inward at a sickening angle, stuck. I held my leg off the ground, continuing to howl until there was nothing left in me. But Johnathan, somehow, stayed the most calm.

A paramedic from the fire truck was the first to arrive; she didn't look at my ankle. Instead, she locked eyes with me, guiding my breath and talking me through it so I wouldn't go into shock.

More paramedics showed up and explained they'd need to cut my shoe off to put an air cast around it before taking me to Harborview, the closest Level 1 trauma center. They cut down the laces and slid the shoe off, twisting it in the same direction my foot was already pointing, which made my forehead go ice cold as sweat poured down my face.

They loaded me onto the gurney and wheeled me off the court and lifted me into an ambulance. Johnathan climbed in right behind me.

When we got to Harborview and they wheeled me out of the ambulance, the cold air from the Puget Sound hit me. A rush of crisp, clean relief cutting through the chaos. It's up there with one of the best feelings I've ever had in my entire life. In the shittiest moments, the few good things you have hit so hard.

Once they put me in a room, they took off the air cast and laid my naked, twisted ankle on the table. It was disgusting. I didn't want to look, but it was my ankle, so I had to. I could see the bottom of my foot without bending my leg.

A doctor walked in, took one look at it, and suddenly nine or ten other doctors, residents, and nurses swarmed the room. They x-rayed me and confirmed it was a subtalar dislocation—the bones under my ankle had slipped out of place. Somehow I hadn't broken anything, the force had been strong enough to pop the bones out cleanly, but now they had to put it back in place.

The team hooked me up to every machine imaginable and prepped me to be put under. The room buzzed with controlled chaos until the head doctor took charge, giving the most direct and confident instructions I've ever heard.

When I woke up, I looked down and saw my toes pointing at the ceiling and started laughing. The dark cloud hanging over me was gone. And once again, Josh, and my friend Evan were there, ready to pick me up from the hospital and take me home.

CHAPTER TWENTY-FOUR

Making It Out

In the days and weeks after, Jazmine visited and spent time with me while I was laid up in my room, unable to move. She didn't need another test, but when she sat through *Rush: Beyond the Lighted Stage* and a Kevin Durant documentary, I knew she really liked me.

It was effortless. We didn't have much in common. She was focused on college, pursuing a career in veterinary medicine, but we loved spending time together. We treated each other with love, respect, and a rare kind of consideration you don't find every day. I admired her so much and was so proud to be associated with her. She became my girlfriend and eventually the day came when we decided to move in together.

There was never a doubt that I wanted to because I had come to love her and saw a future with her, but it hurt to leave Josh and Johnathan at 4755. The sadness in my heart was the same as when I left Mom behind in Goodland. In reality, the situation was different, but my body didn't believe it. I had the same heart-wrenching tension, and I felt heavy, on the verge of tears, even though this time I was only moving a few blocks away. The Rat came with me, starting a new chapter of his life with three cat and two dog siblings.

In 2017, Chris and his wife made plans to visit Seattle. I had looked forward to that day for months, eagerly anticipating their arrival. But when the day finally came, I received a devastating call from my Uncle Rod. He informed me that his oldest brother, my Uncle Mike, had committed suicide.

Mike was living with Grandma and occasionally, he would answer the phone when I called. These brief conversations became a quiet ritual between us. It was unexpected at first, but settled into something comforting. Despite the distance that had existed between us, he never let a call end without telling me he loved me.

A week before his death, while I was busy at work, Mike left me a voicemail. I didn't return his call.

That loss tangled my mind in knots, burdened my soul with the fear of it happening again, making me overthink every interaction with my loved ones, trying to prevent another loss.

Every quiet moment from a loved one came with a risk impossible to ignore. I'd lie awake replaying conversations, searching for warning signs I'd missed, wondering if a single word would change everything. Even a text.

I know Mike didn't take his life because I didn't return his call, but the torment lingers, and self-doubt creeps into my subconscious.

A little before all of this, I started considering getting back into sports journalism. I saw a post from a Twitter account I followed looking for writers, so I took my shot and got accepted as an unpaid intern for a sports website. I was mostly cranking out clickbait headlines and daily pieces on sports and culture, but still, the opportunity was great. And I needed to stay busy. I genuinely enjoyed waking up early, knocking out five stories a day, and watching my Twitter notifications climb when I checked during breaks at my day job.

When the NCAA men's tournament came to Spokane, my boss requested that I cover it. I had to handle my own travel and lodging, but with a media pass and a front-row seat to high-level basketball on the line, I made it work.

I arrived at Veterans Memorial Arena, the lights bright and the stars out. Standing alongside journalists I'd watched on TV, I had the feeling that I'd made something of myself despite turning down that sports director job at the radio station. But I also knew this opportunity was fleeting and I might never get this chance again.

Despite my nerves and inexperience, I took my shots and put myself out there, asking questions at press conferences, interviewing players at their lockers, and soaking up as much as I could.

That experience didn't satisfy me. It left me hungry for more. Finding my way into journalism on my own, this time in a new city, helped build my confidence and self-worth.

Not long after, back in Seattle, I landed a new job working four ten-hour shifts, giving me a three-day weekend every week. With that extra time I started thinking—if my boss could start a website and create these opportunities, why couldn't I build my own?

In 2017, the podcasting industry was growing. With my broadcasting background, I figured I had a decent shot at making it work. So I bought a microphone, did some Googling, and got started.

The first episode was with Kelly and Chris talking about the Cowboys. Naturally. The second was with a friend from work, Gareth, where we went deeper than sports and talked about life and politics. After that, I had a friend from high school who had become a stripper. I kept recording, doing more episodes with Gareth, Kelly, and Chris, but it wasn't enough.

That's when I first had the idea to interview a player from the summer pro-am. I knew landing a current NBA player was a long shot, so I reached out to a familiar local name, Rashaad Powell. He agreed to the interview, and I got to work, researching, writing, and chasing every detail I could find. It was easy, only because I genuinely loved the pro-am.

The interview went as well as I could have hoped. I posted the episode, promoted it on Twitter, and went about my day. I was proud that the show was evolving and that I had made it happen on my own.

After a nice dinner out at University Village, I checked my phone and saw a noti-fication from Twitter: Jamal Crawford retweeted your post. Then I saw that he followed me.

My heart started racing. My mind was spinning, trying to process it. I had to stop myself from spiraling as the possibilities flooded in all at once. Was this really happening?

After talking it over with my brother, I decided to pitch him on making my show the official podcast of the pro-am. It was the longest of long shots. I was some random kid with no real connections, but I put my heart into the message and hit send.

He replied:

"For sure. Come up with a plan, and let's see if we can make it work."

We agreed that I'd cover the player tryouts for the pro-am that year and see how things went.

I prepped my questions and put all that I had into it. My hopes were high, but I was trying to stay grounded, trying not to get ahead of myself.

On the day of the tryouts, I rode my bike along the Burke-Gilman Trail from the U-District to the Royal Brougham Pavilion at Seattle Pacific University. The at-mosphere inside was electric. Everyone was vying for their spot, including me.

I saw Jamal and a few security guys I recognized from past summers, but I kept my distance. I put my bag down, grabbed my mic and recorder, ignored my nerves, and walked up to my first player to ask for an interview. If they had de-clined, my confidence might have crumbled and that would have been it. But they didn't. So I kept going, interview after interview, focusing on building a fun pod-cast episode.

After the tryouts ended, I knew it was my shot to ask Jamal for an interview. It was almost an out-of-body experience. When he agreed, my already heightened nerves shot to another level.

Now I actually had to deliver.

I was shaking, totally unsure if I could get through it, but I had to try. I hit record and, through a shaky voice, introduced the podcast.

"Well, if you've listened to The Jeremy Mills Podcast before, you know I spoke this into existence a couple of weeks ago. I said we were gonna get Jamal Crawford on the podcast, and today is that day. Jamal, welcome."

Jamal laughed through the intro and replied:

"Thank you. I heard it. I listened to it. I actually listened to the edition you did with Rashaad, but you've got a lot of good stuff. I started scrolling down, listening to more and more—and now you're here."

From that moment, he couldn't have been nicer. We connected as people. Later, he told me the reason he gave me a chance was because of how I approached him and presented the idea. He remarked it was the way *he* would have done it.

After finishing the interview that night, I rode my bike down the Burke-Gilman Trail. It was the first and only time in my life I let out a wild yell alone, out of pure joy and total elation.

That summer in 2018, Jamal made me the official podcast of the Seattle pro-am, now dubbed *The CrawsOver*. I requested to have someone with me to help. That was, of course, Johnathan.

Jamal set us up and co-signed us, making it easy to get any interview I wanted. And the Seattle basketball community accepted me faster than I had been anywhere else. The interviews quickly kept getting bigger: Zach LaVine, DeJounte Murray, Tony Wroten, MarJon Beauchamp, Paolo Banchero, Kenny Mayne. And more with Jamal.

It was hard to believe it was happening. Johnathan and I would exchange these looks like, 'Can you believe this is real?'

After the pro-am that summer, Jamal invited us to his invite-only camp for the top 30 high school basketball players in Washington. I recorded interviews there and watched some of the highest-level basketball I'd ever seen. From Tari Eason to Hailey Van Lith. To Isaiah Thomas, Nate Robinson, and Zach LaVine speaking to the kids candidly about the real-life struggles that can come with playing in the league.

Johnathan was tutoring at the time, and Jamal invited him to speak at the camp about education and getting into college. Watching Jamal introduce and endorse him on stage, in front of what would later be multiple future NBA and WNBA players, was somehow even better than when Jamal did it for me.

Somewhere in the middle of all that, Jazmine and I got married.

Earlier that year, on my 25th birthday, I asked Jazmine to marry me. As much as I wanted it, it was one of the hardest things I've ever had to work to say out loud. I could feel the world shifting under my feet, and the future changing, but I got the words out, and she said yes.

We kept the wedding simple. It was just south of Seattle, in Jazmine's best friend's backyard. Having both our families in one place was rare, and it meant a lot. Chris was there too, like he'd been so many times before, showing up for me.

It meant everything to have my brothers and my dad by my side. We'd missed so many milestones over the years, but we got this one. Seeing my dad dressed up in a suit for me helped me feel the weight of the moment.

It was impossible to ignore that my mom wasn't there. But Summer was there to step into that space, so I wouldn't go without a maternal figure.

Not much changed after we got married, since we were already living together. But gaining new family in Jazmine's grandma, her aunt, and her cousins was a pleasant surprise. Every family has its chaos, but compared to what I was used to, spending time with them and watching their dynamic was heartwarming and fascinating in its own way. They spoke more openly to each other, looked out for each other, and their small spats stayed just that—small—without the constant threat of boiling over into chaos and ending relationships. After losing my mom, watching her cousins lean on their mom, argue with her, with each other, let it go and end up back on the couch together at the end of the day, felt almost unreal. A glimpse into a world just out of reach.

Watching them give and receive such unconditional love from their mom so easily reminded me that I would never have that again.

The picture I remember most from our wedding day isn't one where I look particularly handsome. In fact, it's quite the opposite. Seconds before the picture was taken, we had said 'I do' in front of our closest friends and family. Embracing for the first time as husband and wife, I rested my head on her shoulder as if I had melted into her arms. I'm hunched awkwardly, my head almost appearing detached from my body. A wide, uncontrollable grin stretches across my face, with two large veins prominently bulging from my forehead.

This picture captures a moment of triumph after years of struggling without hope that this day would ever come. Years of deep confusion, hurt, and unrelenting manipulation. Yes, I had married someone who brought me immense love and connection, and yet what struck me most in that moment was that I had made it out.

I often saw Mom crying alone on the side of her bed, a flood of dark emotions threatening to drown her. Her eyes were wide and wet, her mouth small and drooping, with wadded-up tissues clenched in her hand.

She was broken.

Broken by her circumstances, by her unrealized and untreated mental health issues. But even at her lowest points, there was talk of making it out, a desperate reach for a hand to pull her from the quicksand of depression. Sometimes, I would try to lift her spirits by talking about better days to come, about us making it out of this life.

Other times, she would bring it up when the darkness and depression had transferred to me. Making it out could mean anything from winning the lottery to simply getting the car to start, beating her addictions, defeating her demons, or reuniting our fractured family.

But she never made it out how I did. She died before she could.

I had everything going for me. Life was turning out better than I ever expected. I had my brothers, my dad, love from my wife, stability, forward motion in my work. But the cold hard reality was no matter what I did, nothing was fixing the effects of my trauma. Not even making it out.

In fact, the closer I got to what I wanted, the clearer it all became.

Somewhere inside of me was still that broken heart, that little boy, crying hysterically into his pillow, desperate for it all to be over. No matter how much time had passed, no matter how far I'd come, he was there.

CHAPTER TWENTY-FIVE

Just Broken

Earlier that same summer, Troy's son Tim passed away from complications related to his lifelong kidney disease. I was grateful that my brothers and I had gone back to Goodland for a family reunion, giving them the chance to see each other one last time. But the reality of it was brutal. Watching Tim deteriorate in front of us, knowing he was dying, was heartbreaking. Someone who had been so full of life and energy was now barely holding on, and clearly not ready to go.

In January 2019, Paul died of a heart attack.

I'd put miles between us. Years, even. But he stayed. Not in person, but in memories and nightmares. Some were loud, screaming memories I couldn't ignore. Others were quiet and hidden deep, but they hurt just as much. We hadn't spoken since I left, but that didn't stop him from haunting me.

When he died, part of me hoped for relief. Maybe, just maybe, the weight of what he left behind would go away. But it didn't.

I felt conflicted, judging myself from both sides. I didn't want to feel happy out of respect for his kids, but I couldn't pretend to feel any grief either. The truth is I didn't know how I felt. And that had always been a problem. After so many years of manipulation and chaos, the part of me that could identify my emotions was gone. It had been a survival mechanism at first, but it never went away.

Even though I knew better, I searched his name on Facebook. I found his profile and started looking through it.

There were photos that looked familiar. First my high school graduation photos. Pictures my family had taken, from a digital camera I used to carry. Pictures from nights I've written about in this book when he insisted on joining in on parties with my friends.

There he was, smiling, posing, archived like a normal man with a normal life. Like none of it ever happened. As if he hadn't torn through my family without remorse. It made me sick to my stomach.

He must've forgotten what he did. But I hadn't.

Part of me hates seeing how easily he was accepted by the Goodland community. Around the time I was in high school, and especially after I left, people had started to treat him as an upstanding citizen.

Despite that, I'm not writing this to drag his name through the dirt. I'm writing this for me. Because I need to get this off of my chest. I need it out of me. I need to say it out loud:

Paul, my feelings toward you are not complicated. Since the day you came into my life, I have had few truly peaceful moments. Not even after you died. I've always kept one eye open. I never wanted you to be part of my story. But you forced your way in. So here you are. This is what you left behind.

After her stroke, when Mom was in the rehabilitation center and we were getting her room set up, I found her cell phone. When I tapped the screen, a new, unread message from Paul showed up. My stomach turned. I didn't know what their relationship was since she left Goodland, and honestly, I didn't want to.

But I opened the message. He had apparently heard about her heart attack and stroke and was begging to see her. He called her a pet name. My stomach turned again.

I scrolled up through their last few messages. It had been a while, and it didn't appear things had ended well between them. This message was him trying to weasel his way in again. Just like he usually did.

It was never about the damage he caused. Never about the misery he left behind. It was never about anything but him feeling good.

But it was too late. I deleted the message and made sure Mom didn't see it.

I finally got to protect her from him.

In February 2022, after enduring the unimaginable grief of burying three of her own children, my grandma passed away at the age of 87.

In a small effort to repay the love she had shown me, I delivered her eulogy, sharing how the unwavering love she gave me will forever define my memories of her. When it came time to go to the cemetery, I had the honor of placing her urn in the ground, giving her one final kiss as I said goodbye.

Her funeral was in early March, not exactly the time of year I would've chosen to return to Goodland. The cold was brutal, the wind sharp enough to cut through layers. You could see it sweeping across the ground in waves. Still, Johnathan and I made the trip.

Aside from burying Grandma, the most meaningful part of that trip was reuniting with Nathan. At some point after I left, he went to live in a group home, so it had been almost ten years since I'd seen him last.

Part of me worried he wouldn't remember me. I wouldn't have blamed him. But he did remember me. He remembered the person I am behind my appearance, better than anyone in Goodland ever has.

He hugged me like he'd missed me. He didn't have to say it. He showed me. Nothing had changed between us. No judgment for leaving. No confusion about how I looked now or the way I spoke. The joy in his eyes said it all. I'm sure mine did too.

The few months after Grandma died, I was not in a great place mentally. The unresolved baggage from my childhood weighed heavily on my heart, and losing four close family members in less than a decade, all before I was thirty, only added more scars. My triggers were quick to get me and slow to let go, dragging me into a deep well of depression that I couldn't climb out of. A depression so heavy it started to pull everything down with it, including my work, my marriage, all of it.

For the past six or seven years, I've been haunted by a recurring nightmare. In it, Mom and I, sometimes joined by my brothers, are desperately rushing to an airport with no warning and no bags, completely unprepared, and on our way to somewhere unknown. It feels less like a choice and more of an escape, as if someone, or something, is forcing us to leave.

The journey to the airport is a harrowing ordeal, speeding past limits, swerving through traffic, gripped by the kind of torment that makes it hard to breathe, even after I wake up.

We face enormous and unbelievable obstacles, as if the universe is conspiring to stop us, and all the while, time is slipping away. When we finally arrive, there's a sudden, terrifying realization: my mom, or someone else on the journey with us, is the one who has to pilot the plane.

As we take off, the atmosphere is charged with a building tension that is reaching its peak. Explosions are erupting behind us, but I realize they are other planes. Each one racing past us, desperately trying to escape a world that seems to be burning.

I didn't remember my dreams every night, but when I did it was *always* that one. Sometimes I'd wake up in the middle of it, heart pounding, freezing from the cold sweat that had soaked my sheets. Other times, I'd wake up in the morning, the emotions of the nightmare lingering, leaving me drained and exhausted before the day had even started.

So, after a long break, I contacted Larry and with his encouragement, I started going to therapy more regularly than I ever had before.

At first, I tried to dodge it. I'd find a reason to reschedule appointments or avoid setting up the next one. But Larry stayed on me. He knew how important it was for me to follow through on this. I hoped that I'd already worked through enough of this to get on with my life, but he knew better.

In the beginning of therapy, it was gratifying enough to speak openly, to finally release the mess of memories, to tell my story fully and honestly to someone who was really listening. And that's where I left it.

But when I returned to it, the real work began—finding the walls I had built to survive, and learning how to knock them down. Because as much as my body didn't believe it, I wasn't just surviving anymore.

When we got in the groove, I started to understand and take advantage of the fact that I had a space where I didn't have to shrink myself to make someone else comfortable, where I didn't have to keep masking, or explaining, or justifying what I felt. I was safe enough to feel honestly.

I started to understand how much of my identity had been shaped around survival, around staying small, staying agreeable, staying quiet. Larry helped me name feelings I'd never had the words for. It helped me understand emotions I'd only ever known as confusion.

Without proper care and with a lot of cold-blooded manipulation from the person who was supposed to love and protect me the most, I was left with feelings I couldn't explain or trust. After years of therapy, and now as an adult, I was able to imagine what had happened to me happening to a random nine-year-old at the grocery store. It broke my heart how clear it made it. What was confusing for so much of my life was now becoming clear. The mistakes my mom had made. The damage that Paul had done to me. I had never known that I was carrying the blame, until I saw it wasn't mine.

In November 2021, I underwent a catheter ablation to address a newly discovered heart condition: supraventricular tachycardia, or SVT. The doctors told me the issue was likely genetic, and I tend to believe them. Larry's not convinced trauma and stress didn't play a part.

The truth is, my heart had been under stress for a long time. Not only physically, but emotionally. Years of tension, anxiety, and existing in survival mode had taken a toll. I didn't realize how much of it I had been carrying in my body until the day I landed in the emergency room, my resting heart rate climbing past 200 beats per minute.

My body was waving a red flag. It couldn't take the panic, the racing thoughts, or the constant inability to rest.

After the surgery, recovery wasn't only about healing the small incision from the procedure. It was about learning how to actually care for myself. To listen to my body and to slow down.

I had to learn that self-care wasn't selfish. That rest wasn't laziness. That my heart wasn't broken because it was weak. It was just broken.

Overall, therapy has been the biggest reason for my mental health improvement. The consistency of therapy helped me beyond anything I ever hoped for. Now, when I get triggered, whether it's a picture of my mom, a song, or a woman on TV crying or screaming, I'm able to recover more quickly. I don't stay stuck in that dark place as long. What sunk deep into my bones is slowly surfacing, bit by bit, as if my body is finally ready to let it go.

Jazmine's unwavering love has been a constant source of strength, and I'm incredibly proud of our marriage. She has seen me at my worst and most torn apart, trying to process all of this. Neither of us had the best examples growing up, so building the relationship that we have is one of my greatest accomplishments. Even though they never met, and to be completely honest, Jazmine has her reservations about Mom, she extends a hand of peace by wearing a pair of her old earrings and her blue denim fanny pack as a tribute. That means the world to me.

Meditation, daily journaling, and revisiting the darkest moments of my life in the early hours of the morning while writing and rewriting this memoir have also accelerated my progress.

And now, as a testament to that progress, for nearly two years now, my recurring nightmare hasn't returned.

CHAPTER TWENTY-SIX

In the End

After spending nine years apart from my brothers after they left Kansas, I was lucky enough to spend exactly nine years with them in Seattle. I only left when my wife was accepted into veterinary school in the Phoenix area—a brief four-year hiatus before we returned home to Seattle in 2024.

Early on when I returned to Seattle, I gave my brothers an early draft of this book, which stirred up a lot of emotions, but their pride in me was impossible to miss. It sparked conversations in which we were able to truly express what had gone unexpressed for so long. Our most closely guarded feelings about ourselves, how we saw each other, and the admiration of each other's strengths.

That night, we all went out together to Capitol Hill, ending up at a bar. It was a busy Saturday night, standing room only, with people crowded all around. But through the noise and chaos, we created a force field around ourselves, and it was as if the rest of the world ceased to exist. We spoke from the deepest parts of our hearts, tears flowing freely. Our drinks sat untouched, the ice melting, as we remained locked into each other's words, oblivious to everything around us.

We shared conversations about our shared trauma, individual traumas, and experiences that we never imagined we'd have the strength or understanding to confront or share with each other. It was the most important conversation of my life. In that moment, we shattered an invisible barrier that had held back so many before us, stunting their growth.

I catch myself looking at them, remembering how deeply I longed for them, and how incredible it is that we're here together. They've grown into great men, and greater brothers.

Johnathan's hair is still dark brown, and frames a kind, innocent face, with blue eyes that are now unburdened, still giving him an air of warmth and thoughtfulness. He's still known as the smart one, but the empathy and caring he has developed over the years sticks out to me most. His principles continue to be strong, and he is as well-read as anyone I know. If you met him, you might believe he's quiet, but with Josh and me, he's anything but.

Josh's hair is still dark too, softly curled, and as wild as ever. His eyes are deep brown, mischievous and now hopeful, framed with rounded glasses. Tall and lanky, he wears his signature mustache and the classic army jacket from Goodwill that has held up for going on fifteen years now. Whatever it is that makes us who we are as a Mills, Josh still has the most of it and in its purest form. He's one of the few people in the world who can surprise me, say something truly unexpected, and recommend things I end up falling in love with, especially music.

They, along with my dad, are the only people on earth I relate to at my very core. The only ones I can truly understand, and who truly understand me.

As brothers, we've built our own world, shaped by a decade of shared experiences, mutual understanding, and the kind of rapport that only comes from life spent together. It means everything to me.

As brothers, we've rebuilt our relationship into what it should've been all along. And beyond that. We reconnected, grew together, and had fun. But now, we've taken our bond to a level none of us could've imagined. We talk openly about our feelings, about the past, the present, and whatever might be coming next.

That night at the bar, it was hard not to envision how proud the mom who read to us and told us sweet dreams every night would have been.

After all these years and all the miles between us, Kelly, Chris, and I have stayed as close as can be. There is rarely a day when our group chat is quiet. They both ended up in Nebraska, married with kids, becoming solid foundations for their families. And somehow, we've managed to find time for each other through it all.

Most recently, we met up in Dallas to catch a Cowboys game at AT&T Stadium— the same team we spent so many childhood Sundays watching together. It was triumphant to stand there together, taking it all in.

The day before the game, we toured the stadium and played catch on the field. We'd finally reached the place we'd been chasing for years.

After one of the hardest weeks of writing this book, as I relived the painstaking details of the hardest days of my life, Josh and I took a short drive north of Seattle to visit Dad.

Sitting with him at lunch, I could feel his energy healing my hurt. I didn't bring up what I was writing about, but my body didn't care. It soaked up the comfort of my father's presence. He's in his seventies now, and at his core, still the same person I knew growing up. I just know him a lot better now. His beard is big and white, and he's as wise as ever. Somehow, he's always right. Especially when I think he's not.

It's taken years of hard work to finally reach a place where I can be honest about my mom, not only to others, but myself. While yes, it hurts to speak of her this way, I've come to realize it's not my fault that this is my story.

Yes, she loved me, but she also hurt me. A lot. She wasn't able to resolve her own inner turmoil, and she ruthlessly manipulated me, knowingly and repeatedly making choices that placed me in harmful situations that would take me a decade to work through—not that I will ever be truly finished.

This was the reality I was given, and facing it head-on is a final step toward healing myself.

With the clarity of an adult mind, I've come to terms with the fact that what happened was deeply wrong, and those responsible bear the weight of that.

But I also love my mom so much and cherish her memory. I love her as much as a son can love his mother. If I ever get to see her again in some sort of afterlife, I'll hug her until my arms go numb. And I won't feel ashamed for sharing my story.

But I can't say that sometimes my heart doesn't hurt. Because I just miss her.

I can no longer shield her from the truth when it will set me free.

And with that, I'm taking another step to set this burden free. The weight of this story is no longer only mine to bear. And it won't die with me.

The mom I had before everything fell apart, the one who raised me in a loving home and taught me so much in my first five years, that mom would have wanted this for her boy. She would have wanted me to find this freedom, and to no longer carry her burdens.

The silence, just eating it, day after day, has a cost. It distorts your sense of worth. You start to lose trust in yourself, and in the foundation of the world around you. It keeps you hesitant and pulls you away from living life uninhibited. And who knows what kind of effect it has on your health.

I've shared a lot of pain in this book. But I'm okay now. However, I bet someone in your life isn't. And they could use that sympathy, so I encourage you to seek them out, look for signs they are struggling, and offer help with as gentle a hand as you can.

In the grand scheme of everything Goodland has witnessed—the violence, the death, the silence, the generations of hurt—my story might not seem like much. But it was real. It left a mark. And now, it's part of the record.

I will close with one more story about Mom, the way I like to picture her when I think of her now.

During my senior year of high school, Mom and I took a slow drive on a sunny day out in the rural country around Goodland, eventually making our way out to Smoky Gardens. Just us two. It was special from the moment she asked me to go.

It was a peaceful, reflective afternoon for both of us. We didn't say much, but we didn't need to. In the silence, we both understood that we were fully enjoying each other's presence. A rare peace, where having each other close was enough.

The car's tires crunched softly over the dirt road, a familiar, comforting sound. The gentle vibration beneath us and the scent of dust hanging in the air, trailing behind, grounded us in the moment. Sunlight streamed through the windshield, warming our legs, as the quiet connection between mother and son deepened without a word.

We were quietly happy.

We made it out to the Smoky, Mom's favorite place in the entire world. She absorbed the energy and shared it with me, telling me stories of her childhood as she pointed out different landmarks. Like the time her dad put on a Halloween mask and crept outside her bedroom window to scare her and Terri, or where they would spot the elusive mountain lion every few months. She also shared tales of wanderers getting into trouble while fishing and the impressive ways her dad would take care of them.

The Smoky was her happy place in a world where she felt so much agony. It softened her. She cherished the memories of growing up, and especially while her dad was still around.

We talked, and listened, enjoying the simple, quiet nature of where she had grown up. I brought my digital camera along that day, and before we left, we drove to the south side of the Smoky and took pictures of each other. I stood by the lake. When it was her turn, she jumped up into one of the big trees her dad had planted all those years earlier, and stood proudly.

And then we sat in the shade and had a rest, one last time.